# "YOUR BOY, JIM": THE DIARY AND LETTERS OF A SOLDIER IN WORLD WAR I

By

Alexander R. Foy

# ABSTRACT

This thesis aims to tell the story of James Austin Bowman as he navigated the Western Front during World War I. The thesis utilizes two main types of historical documents: the personal diary and the letters to his wife. During his time on the Western Front, Bowman wrote in a personal diary about the uncertainty and daily life of a soldier inching closer to war. Bowman also wrote over forty-three letters to his wife, Evelyn, as he shared his thoughts and emotions while the world was at war. For one hundred years, my family has preserved these historical documents. The thesis will use the diary and letters of James Bowman as main primary sources along with a variety of secondary sources on trauma, memory, and World War I.

The first chapter introduces James Bowman and history regarding his early life and the lifechanging move to California. This chapter aims to analyze the diary within the story of James Bowman and the 91st Division. The second chapter allows the diary to serve as a guide to retell the story of James Bowman as the 91st Division inched closer to the Meuse Argonne Offensive. The third chapter examines a small but revealing and representative portion of the letters that James wrote to Evelyn on the Western Front. The letters offer a glimpse into their relationship as a newly married couple and how open he is to be sharing his thoughts and emotions during the fight of his life. The fourth chapter examines the impact of war on my family and how James Bowman's experience during World War I affected his family in shaping their worldview.

# TABLE OF CONTENTS

# LIST OF FIGURES

## Figure

# CHAPTER 1

## INTRODUCTION

In the dark, they have been sitting there, locked away. In boxes, they have traveled from one home to the next. As they were passed down to their children, they were taken out once only to be put away and divided again into plastic bins. Still they sat there, locked away. In these bins, located in two separate parts of the home, were the thoughts, emotions, and words of a shy, reserved man. One bin contained a golden shoe box with his most prized possessions from that moment in time. In that bin contained a small notebook of his deepest thoughts and emotions that he only expressed to an audience of one, himself. In the other bin, folded into neat stacks of paper in a larger brown shoe box was his greatest gift of all. This other bin contained his love for the only other person in the world that completed him as a person. Each of these bins held the key to a moment in time. A moment that has been locked away until today. The words on these pages have been kept shut for nearly a century until now. The words that were hidden for so long in a frayed black journal and mismatched YMCA stationary were written by a United States Army private during World War I. These words were written by my great-grandfather, James Austin Bowman.

Six years ago, I was sitting on my grandparents' living room couch discussing my summer school class on World War I. My mom had asked my grandfather a question regarding whether he had anything left over from his father's time during the war. With this simple question asked by my mother, it launched an investigation into my great-grandfather's past and the findings of the diary. A few years later, in a spring cleaning of my grandparent's house, I would soon discover my great-grandfather's letters written to Evelyn, my great-grandmother. These two historical documents would become the focal point of this thesis.

The thesis will examine these two historical documents by placing them in context of the Great War. In the second chapter, I will examine James's war experience through his diary and how he changed throughout the events of the war. The chapter contains the entire diary from start to finish as James begins his journey during World War I. Secondary sources will help give context to the path of

James's journey with the 364th Infantry as they drill, march, and fight on the Western Front. The diary is an important historical document because it allows us to connect with James through a private channel. James's diary is unique because it allows us to catch a glimpse of his experience in real time during the events of the war. Even though James's diary is private and personal, it is different from the modern concepts of diaries. Modern diaries are private and meant for the eyes of solely one person but James's World War I diary was meant to be read. In the diary, James would discuss the day's events in a communal aspect, like "we marched 9 miles" or "we had dinner." James's diary was not meant to be completely private for the outside world and it could give us clues to why he kept it after the war had ended.

The third chapter will analyze the letters what James had written to his wife Evelyn. The collection of letters starts at the beginning of his service on the Western Front in July and continue throughout his journey until he arrives back safely in New York in April. The letters reveal the many aspects of James's personality that begin to change as the war continues. James discusses the mundane events of the training and marching to the Front. He discusses his future life whenever he returns home. After the Meuse Argonne Offensive, James begins to question the higher authorities in his life which reflect a loss of innocence from the man that left Camp Lewis. The letters are also a personal connection between the couple by giving the reader an insight to how they navigated their relationship three thousand miles apart. The letters and diary also work together to show what James shares with his wife and what he omits from his diary. The letters contain detail and length which will show the drastic difference between his motivation to write letters compared to the diary.

The diary and letters are important documents to analyze in how they were preserved for so many years. The diary was preserved in a golden shoe box that sustained itself during multiple moves from one house to the next. Out of all the items from the war, James decided to keep the diary, a mirror, a bar of soap, and a map of France. Within these items, there are no letters from Evelyn. James decided to keep the diary because it had a significant amount of meaning to him from the war. The diary contained a piece of James's experience that he could not discard. The letters written to Evelyn were preserved in their original envelopes. James did not save Evelyn's letters written to him while he was on the Western Front. There could have been a variety of reasons why James did not keep her letters. He could have lost them in battle or misplaced them when he was discarding extra weight during their marches to the Front. The diary and letters complement each other in understanding both James the soldier and James the husband. The letters and diary also work together to show what James shares with his wife and what he omits from his diary. It shows the drastic difference between his motivation to write letters compared to the diary.

The fourth chapter will examine the legacy of James Bowman. The fourth chapter will analyze the relationship between James and his son, Robert. It will discuss Robert's own experience with the United States Army and how his father's service impacted his experience. The chapter will also analyze the legacy of patriotism within the family and how James passed down the characteristic of fulfilling a duty to your country. The chapter will also analyze how his war experience affected his family well after his time in the United States Army. James's legacy was not only wrapped up in the Great War, but it was found in his steadfast devotion to take care of his family through the end.

# James Austin Bowman

James Austin Bowman was born on September 30, 1887, in the small town of Sandy Lake, Pennsylvania to Joseph Gilbert Bowman and Amanda Emma Bowman (Borland). Sandy Lake is a small town located in the northwest of Pennsylvania, about 70 miles away from the city of Pittsburgh. The Bowman family had moved from New York in the 1810s to Mercer County, Pennsylvania. The family resided in the region for the next one hundred and thirty years. In the 1880s, Sandy Lake had a small population of 730 according to the 1880 United States Census.[1] Mercer County was home to a population of around 67,000 in 1880.[2] The region has a predominantly small, rural landscape. In this small, rural community, the Bowmans began to learn the traits of hard work and grit.

James was the youngest of five children: Robert Emmerson (1877-1900), Charles Gilbert (1880-1970), Kathryn Blanche (1882-1950), Samuel Joseph (1885-1972), and James Austin (1887-1972).

---

[1] United States Census Bureau. *Census of Population and Housing, 1880: Statistics of the Population of the United States*. (Washington, D.C: U.S. Government Printing Office, 1880).

[2] United States Census Bureau. *Census of Population and Housing, 1880: Statistics of the Population of the United States*. (Washington, D.C: U.S. Government Printing Office, 1880).

Samuel, known in my family as Uncle Sam, was the closest to James. Kathryn, known as Aunt Kit, was also a close confidant to the youngest child. James's grandfather, Joseph A. Bowman, was a preacher at Cumberland Presbyterian Church in Mercer County. The Bowman family had a deep connection to the Presbyterian community and the Bowman children were raised Presbyterian.

Tragedy had struck James early in his life when his mother, Amanda Bowman, died when he was seven years old. In 1908, James's father was later married to Elizabeth Jackson, who had three children of her own from a previous relationship. The loss of his mother created a hole within his life which may have sprung him into his mischievous ways in his early childhood. From stories by Uncle Sam and Aunt Kit that were passed down to my grandfather, James was mischievous in the classroom.[3] Being the youngest of five children, he was known as the troublemaker of the family.[4] Some psychologists and sociologists would cite losing his mother so early in life as one of the reasons for his bad behavior in the classroom and the lack of motivation for an education. From an oral

---

[3] Robert Bowman, interview by Alexander Foy, February 2017.

[4] Robert Bowman, interview by Alexander Foy, February 2017.

history of my grandfather, it is believed that James never made it past either the fourth or seventh grade.[5] He did not attend high school or ever receive his G.E.D. later in life. Information from the period between the 1890s and 1914 are lost because of the lack of evidence or sharing on the part of my great-grandparents.

In 1915, James Austin Bowman boarded a train headed for California and his story was just about to begin. His brother, Sam, had written to him earlier in the year that the oil fields in Fellows, California were hiring and if he wanted to make the move, he should make the trip out west. As James and Sam ventured out to Fellows, California and became settled, there was a nineteen-year-old daughter of a dairy farmer getting ready to move again. Evelyn Tilden, the daughter of Marshall and Eva, was born on December 16, 1896 in Los Angeles, California. Marshall Tilden was born in Oxford, Ohio, but soon moved with his parents Dr. Daniel Tilden and Adaline Tilden to Osborne County, Kansas. Like the Bowmans, the Tilden family had a knack for exploring and living in the middle of nowhere. The Tilden family also attempted to make a foundation of their own in the middle of nowhere, Kansas.

---

[5] Robert Bowman, interview by Alexander Foy, November 2017.

Marshall Tilden married Eva Knox in 1877 and they moved to Southern California in the late 1890s. Marshall was known for creating a dairy business and then quickly moving to the next prosperous location. The family would move from Los Angeles to Kern County to Turlock then back to Kern County until finally settling in Long Beach for the final years of their life. From Turlock, as a teenager, Evelyn starred on the Turlock High School basketball team. Before the beginning of her senior year, the Tilden family made one of their signature moves moving from Turlock to Fellows, California in the mid-1910s.

With both James and Evelyn in Fellows, California, the love story begins in a small dance hall. Like the shot heard round the world in the American Revolution, it is unknown who made the first move, who talked first, but soon enough they would begin a relationship that would last nearly fifty years. After a few short months of dating, James Bowman and Evelyn Tilden were married on August 14, 1917. James had established himself as a laborer for the oil industry with the South Pacific Oil Company and then with K. T. O. Oil Company and Evelyn worked as a preschool aide.

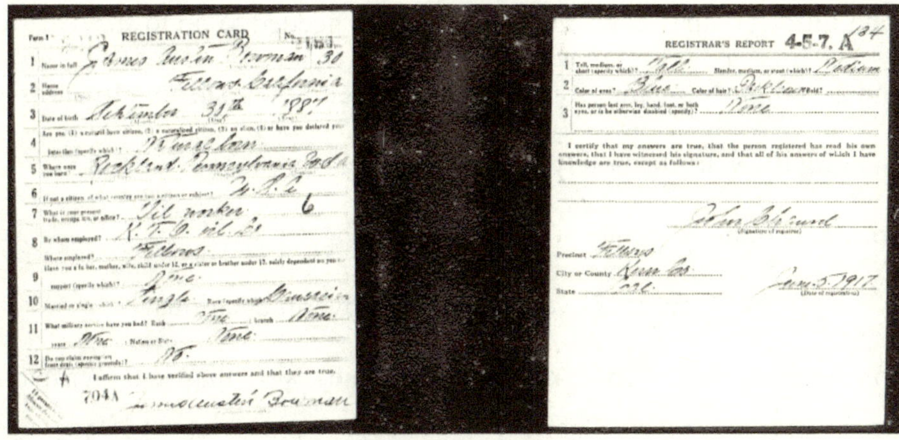
REGISTRATION CARD

1 Name in full: James Austin Bowman 30

2 Home address: Fellows California

3 Date of birth: September 31st 1887

5 Where were you born: Rockland Pennsylvania U.S.A.

7 What is your present trade, occupation, or office? Oil worker

8 By whom employed? Fellows

10 Married or single: Single

11 What military service have you had? None

I affirm that I have verified above answers and that they are true.

James Austin Bowman

REGISTRAR'S REPORT 4-5-7. A

1 Tall, medium, or short (specify which)? Tall. Slender, medium, or stout (which)? Medium

2 Color of eyes? Blue. Color of hair? Black

3 Has person lost arm, leg, hand, foot, or both eyes, or is he otherwise disabled (specify)? None

I certify that my answers are true, that the person registered has read his own answers, that I have witnessed his signature, and that all of his answers of which I have knowledge are true, except as follows:

(Signature of registrar)

Precinct: Fellows

City or County: Kern Co.

State: Cal.

June 5 1917 (Date of registration)

*Figure 1.* James Austin Bowman's World War I Selective Service Paperwork[6].

Nearly two months before their marriage, James was summoned by the United States government to register for the draft. On June 5, 1917, the twenty-nine-year-old oil laborer had ventured to the local office in Fellows, California, and filled out a draft card.[7] James was not married yet, nor did he have any prior military service. James could be defined as just an average man. He was tall, medium build. An oil worker with no education and relatively no money. James fit into the mold of the United States Army, someone

---

6 Ancestry.com. U.S., WORLD WAR I DRAFT REGISTRATION CARDS, 1917-1918 [database on-line]. Provo, UT, USA: Ancestry.com Operations Inc, 2005.

7 United States, Selective Service System. WORLD WAR I SELECTIVE SERVICE SYSTEM DRAFT REGISTRATION CARDS, 1917-1918. (Washington, D.C.: National Archives and Records Administration, 1918). M1509, 4,582 rolls. Imaged from Family History Library microfilm.

who followed directions and did what they needed to do to survive and accomplish the mission. With the United States shifting towards entering the war, the newly married couple, were faced with an uncertain future.

In 1917, another event was taking over the national conversation. A few short months before they were married, German U-boats had been attacking and sinking United States merchant ships in the Atlantic Ocean. A war that had been raging on for the last three years in Europe was no longer avoidable for the neutral United States. James Bowman would enter the United States as a Private in Company F in the 364$^{th}$ Infantry of the 91$^{st}$ Division in the American Expeditionary Force.

Before we begin in accompanying James with his journey on the Western Front in the Great War, we must first learn who James was as a person. Of course, this profile is hard to build from a man that I never met and has been dead for over 46 years. But one of the best gifts that I have is the opportunity to look at James through the eyes of his son, Robert. James was a relatively tall man. He was six foot two inches with long legs and a somewhat of a well-built body; he was not over or underweight. James carried the Bowman hairline: a widow's peak in the front of the head that pushed his hairline back by the time he reached the age of 30. The Bowman hairline has been passed down through generations. I guess I can find a point of pride in losing my hair at an early age. Yet, James's tall stature hid his shy and reserved personality.

James was shy. It was the first thing my family would always bring up when describing him. As my grandfather describes him, he was one of those people that would be in the back of the dinner party and you might have never known he attended.[8] He kept to himself and, like my grandfather, was a man of few words. He was calculated with his speech, a trait that has been passed down to his son. James was known as being shy and soft spoken even after he exited the Army in 1919. My grandfather, Robert Bowman, remembers his father as being incredibly shy and soft spoken. "He was very soft spoken. I would say, he just wanted the best for his family and it's kind of hard to explain because he didn't do a lot of talking."[9] The shy and quiet nature of James is important to note when analyzing how he communicates through the letters with

---

[8] Robert Bowman, interview by Alexander Foy, November 2017.

[9] Robert Bowman, interview by Alexander Foy, November 2017.

Evelyn and through the diary with himself. Each person has a unique way of expressing themselves either through writing, talking, or non-verbal actions. James finds ways to discuss his experience with Evelyn when trying to make sense of the war. Writing could have been a good use of therapy to move on from the terror of war.

James's shy nature also allowed him to be known as gentle to his family members. "Gentle" is the most common word I have heard over the course of my interviews and conversations when describing Bowman men, whether it be James or my grandfather Robert. He was known as being soft-spoken and gentle. In an interview with my grandfather, he described his father as a "He was very shy. He wouldn't speak up on a lot of conversations, he would just listen . . . He was shy, very shy, not outgoing, he sort of kept to himself a lot."[10] My mother as expresses the same sentiment regarding James Bowman, as she remembers her grandfather be very kind and gentle. After reflecting and critically thinking about my family history, I believe the shy and gentle nature is a personality trait that has been passed along through generations of Bowmans.

---

[10] Robert Bowman, interview by Alexander Foy, November 2017.

Mercer County was known as a small, rural community. It was where James would spend most of his childhood, teenage and early adult years of his life. It was home where he learned and practiced his blue-collar roots. James's new home in Kern County was similar in the size and landscape of Mercer County. James had taken the toughness he learned in Pennsylvania and applied it to the fields of California. After the war was over, James and Evelyn lived in various homes in Kern County, moving from job to job. Once the Great Depression hit, the Bowman family, like the rest of the country, suffered hardship in the face of extreme poverty. James and Evelyn moved the family from Kern County to Long Beach, California, where they would raise their three children, James, Betty, and Robert.[11] James worked in a variety of roles within the oil industry and eventually became a farmer in the mid-1930s near Downey, California. In the diary, James refers to buying a house to raise his future family. Although he did raise that family, the family was never able to buy the home after World War I and with the Great Depression it was a hard reality for James and Evelyn.

---

[11] United States Census Bureau. *Census of Population and Housing, 1930: Statistics of the Population of the United States*. (Washington, D.C: U.S. Government Printing Office, 1930).

According to my grandfather, his family was always considered lower middle class with having barely enough money to get by.

The third characteristic of his personality is what my grandfather would refer to as the unwritten rule of the Bowman way. Through the oral interviews and the twenty-five years of knowing my grandfather, I have realized that the Bowmans have a creed of doing what needs to be done. In my oral interviews, my grandfather would refer to the creed of doing what needs to be done when talking about his father.[12] I believe that his unwritten rule was developed over years of hard labor and tough financial situations. From the small rural town of Sandy Lake, Pennsylvania, to the barren central valley of California, James was a product of this tough and small-town environment. Working in the oil industry hardens a man in a different way than working in finance or a desk job. It takes a certain type of person to dive deep into the Earth's surface to dig out some coal or line up pipes to drill oil.

Throughout his life, James Bowman was never a manager or someone who led a group on the job. This fact was due in large part to his shy personality but perhaps also the fact that he worked better

[12] Robert Bowman, interview by Alexander Foy, November 2017.

as a follower rather than a leader. This idea of doing what needs to be done even when you are not a leader would be referred to as grit. Grit is defined as a "firmness of mind or spirit and an unyielding courage in the face of hardship or danger."[13] James was always in the position of stepping up to the challenge of whatever needs to be done, whether it's a difficult project or storming a German machine gun nest. James carried this mentality throughout his life and like many other things passed it down to my grandfather and my mother. Combined with the shy, passive, and gentle personality, James was more than willing to shut up and work because that is what needed to be done.

If my great-grandfather was anything like his son, Robert (my grandfather), I know that he was a gentle, quiet, and strong man. He was steadfast in his commitment to defend his loved ones and the country he loved. Many of the lessons that I have been taught from my grandfather were an extension from James himself. The unwritten rule was also accompanied by belief in religion and how one person should conduct himself. My great-grandfather was known as a religious man. He refers to his faith many times

---

[13] Meriam-Webster Dictionaries, s.v. "grit" accessed September 12, 2019, https://www.merriam-webster.com/dictionary/grit.

throughout the diary. My grandfather refers to James as a "God-fearing man" but he never went to church. James's religious experience was more of a personal journey through discussion and reading the Scripture than going to Sunday Service. Although he was infrequent in attending Presbyterian mass, James was still deeply rooted in his faith. My great-grandfather was known as a man to live by the Golden Rule.[14] "Do to others what you want them to do to you."[15] The Golden Rule was how James believed life should be lived. The Golden Rule was the guiding principle for my great-grandfather and tested his foundation as a human amid chaos. The Golden Rule would also test James in the most trying moments of his life. When faced with the adversity of war and the possibility of ending a life, the Golden Rule must have created an internal conflict on how humans should treat its fellow humankind. War and religion places itself in an uncompromising position. When one is taught to love one another, where do you place your enemy?

---

[14] Robert Bowman, interview by Alexander Foy, November 2017.

[15] The Bible, Matthew 7:12.

## Historical Documents

As I stated earlier, the diary, along with the letters have been hidden away in the dark, resting for nearly ninety-five years, as they traveled from household to household waiting for the right moment to breach the light of day. By the time I began writing this thesis, it had approached the 100$^{th}$ anniversary of World War I and there the documents remained locked away never seeing the light of day or having enthusiastic eyes to view it. This project began with a simple question in the summer of 2014. Sitting on the tan couch in the spare bedroom of my grandparent's house, I asked the question one summer weekend afternoon, "Do you know if there is anything of great grandpas from World War I?" I was taking a summer school class in the History Department. My grandfather would find this golden shoe box in the closet and would launch the next six years of investigating the journey of my great-grandfather.

After receiving my acceptance into the American Studies graduate program, I already knew my plan for the thesis and how I was going to execute this research project. I was sitting on an academic gold mine that was too good to pass up. Some researchers wait their entire life for a break, and, for me, it was sitting in a golden shoe box surrounded by a bar of soap, a map of France, and a mirror. When returning to the material I deemed boring a few summers ago, the dry PowerPoints had transformed and were replaced with words, ideas, and thoughts from my own flesh and blood. In research, sometimes one must search for history and on the other hand sometimes history finds you. My great-grandfather probably never meant for me to pick up the diary and letters, transcribe it, then write it into a larger project, and then publish it for others. For one hundred years, history was waiting to emerge from its slumber and James Bowman finally presented himself to the modern world.

## World War I

The beginning of the Great War has often been romanticized as the assassination that catapulted the world in war. On June 28, 1914, nearly four years before James began his trip to the Western Front, a young Bosnian terrorist named Gavrilo Princip assassinated Archduke Franz Ferdinand and his wife, Sophie. Archduke Franz Ferdinand was the heir to the Austro-Hungarian throne and the assassination began a ripple effect of tensions within the European region. The assassination was no way the ultimate cause for Europe to go to war, but it was a fuse that began a long chain of events that culminated in the world going to war.

On July 28, 1914, after failed negotiations and an ultimatum, Austria-Hungary declared war on Serbia. Germany aligned itself with Austria-Hungary and France united with Russia and then eventually Britain. Paul Fussell puts the great war into perspective, showing how a small event caused great destruction in most of Europe. "In the Great War eight million people were destroyed because two persons, the Archduke and his Consort, had been shot."[16] With the countries mobilized for war, the generals of the combatant countries were eager and more than willing to test military plans that they had spent years crafting. The Great War would wrap numerous countries and millions of men into a fight of degradation and destruction.

While the British and the French began fighting in 1914, the United States had been promoting a sense of neutrality which was led by President Wilson. For years, the United States avoided war and Wilson was reelected on his promise that "He kept us out of the

---

[16] Paul Fussell. *The Great War and Modern Memory*. Oxford Univ. Press Pbk. ed. Galaxy Book; GB483. London; New York: Oxford University Press, 1977, 9.

War."[17] But as the death toll of French and British troops began to rise, the United States decided to help its allies with more manpower. Due to the United States reluctance to intervene in the War, the country was unprepared to fight, both in trained military and with machinery. In American popular culture, the sinking of the *Lusitania* is the one event that is seared into the minds of Americans as the tipping point that eventually led us into the war. In May 1915, the *Lusitania* was sunk off the coast of Ireland by German submarines, which prompted outrage from the American government that threatened to go to war against Germany.[18] During the time of 1915-1916, President Woodrow Wilson "spent two years in an extensive effort to make himself the mediator between the opposed coalitions, hoping that the war would end without requiring American belligerency."[19] After these negotiations fell through, President Wilson chose to intervene and decided to join the British and French. With Germany, unrelenting on their unrestrictive

---

[17] Saladin Ambar, "Woodrow Wilson: Campaigns and Elections," Miller Center, University of Virginia, September 12, 2019, https://millercenter.org/president/wilson/campaigns-and-elections.

[18] Hew Strachan. *The First World War*. Oxford [England]; New York: Oxford University Press, 2001, 128.

[19] Hew Strachan. *The First World War*, 210.

submarine warfare and other dominoes falling in foreign policy, the United States aligned itself with the Allied Powers.

The Western Front was one setting for this global war that rested near the eastern border of France and included parts of Belgium. The Germans adopted the von Schlieffen Plan that was created by General Alfred von Schlieffen in 1905. The plan was an aggressive maneuvering of the German army to invade the French from the north and sweep down into Paris and head west by defeating the heavily fortified French. Once the German forces had taken out the French troops, they would then use the highly advanced rail line to make their way to the Eastern Front to take off the slowly mobilizing Russians.[20] This plan required many dominoes to fall into place, especially with Germany marching into neutral countries Belgium, Luxemburg, and the Netherlands. But as World War I would slowly unfold, the old von Schlieffen Plan did not account for the modern machinery that would envelop the battlefield in 1915. Germany had launched their offensive in August 1914 against France by invading Belgium to carry out their version of the von Schlieffen Plan. With the invasion of neutral Belgium, it had

---

[20] Browder, Dewey. "Schlieffen Plan." World War I: The Definitive Encyclopedia and Document Collection, 2014, 1430-432.

given the British a "cast-iron excuse for intervention" and eventually led to the British entering the war.[21] For two years, the countries would be locked in a stalemate, gaining or losing four hundred yards or a mile at a time. By 1915, the Allied forces estimated that they maintained 15,000 miles of trenches along the Western Front.[22] It took nearly three years for the Great War to finally have some movement with the introduction of the United States military to this global war. With the world at war for nearly three years, James Bowman and the rest of the United States military answered the nation's call to restore peace to the global stage.

---

[21] Norman Stone. *World War One*. New York: Basic Books, a Member of the Perseus Books Group, 2009, 28.

[22] Jennifer Keene, *American Soldiers' Lives: World War I*. Westport, CT; Greenwood Press, 2006, 135.

# CHAPTER 2

"LOOK OUT BOCHE"

## The Journey Begins

Situated in the evergreen forest of the Pacific Northwest, the sound of a bugle fills the air as men begin training one cold, foggy afternoon. Stomping boots hit the dirt in a small section of what would make up the seventy thousand acres that would eventually become Camp Lewis. A former National Guard training camp, the United States government selected the site and began to erect barracks for a huge camp that would train men for World War I. On September 8, 1917, among the unfinished two-story buildings, the first men arrived at Camp Lewis, which would become home of the United States Army's 91st Division.

Comprised of men from the eight Western states, the 91st Division was formed under the direction of Major General H. A. Greene. As the organizational structure began to take shape, the 91st

Division was designated into two infantry brigades, 181st and 182nd, and three artillery regiments, 346th, 347th, and 348th. The 364th Infantry was formed out of the 182nd brigade and would be the future home of James Bowman for the entirety of the war.

After arriving to an unfinished camp, the men of Camp Lewis "found it in a very rough and unfinished condition with a lack of anything resembling paved roads or sidewalks" and the lack of paved roads created a desert of dust due to the heavy traffic.[23] This description comes from Bryant Wilson and Lamar Tooze's informative account of the 364th Infantry from the start of basic training to the end of the War.[24] The barracks and the unpaved roads were one aspect of Camp Lewis that new recruits of the 91st Division had to bear but there was one factor that the majority Southern Californians were shocked to experience in the Pacific Northwest, the rain. California, known for its sunny beaches and great weather, never experienced the amount of rainfall that the Pacific Northwest offers to its residents. The major obstacle for many was getting used

---

[23] Bryant Wilson and Lamar Tooze. *With the 364th Infantry in America, France and Belgium*. (New York: The Knickerbocker Press, 1919), 3.

[24] Bryant Wilson served a First Lieutenant and Chaplain and Lamar Tooze served a First Lieutenant and Regimental Intelligence Officer in the 364th Infantry.

to the rainy season and the gloom that would arrive with the clouds. The rain would serve as a test and simulation for life on the Front, beginning the long ride of gloom and doom for many soldiers.

It had been nearly 20 years since the United States had entered a war, the last being the Spanish-American War which began on April 25, 1898 and ended by December 1898. The only blueprint for many American soldiers was a war that ended within a year. Officers in the United States Army believed that discipline and skills were developed through a long-term process of two years.[25] "Ideally, a new recruit would receive four months of rudimentary instruction in basic soldier skills in 'companies of instruction' conducted at a recruit depot--David Island, NY or Columbus Barracks, OH, for Infantry--before joining his unit."[26] But with the heightened escalation of war, the Army was faced with issues of replacing men on the front lines with trained recruits. The period of World War I saw basic instruction for new soldiers drastically reduced from four months to 36 workings days (approximately six weeks) because

---

[25] Roger K. Spickelmier, "Training of the American Soldier During World War I and World War II." PhD. diss., U.S. Army Command and General Staff College, 1987, 21.

[26] Spickelmier, "Training of the American Soldier During World War I and World War II," 21-22.

officials believed that a shorter training would result in better management of the replacement flow to the Front.[27] With the Army' adaptation to the current climate of the War, James was rushed into an accelerated training program to prepare him for life in the trenches. James Bowman enlisted into the United States Army on October 2, 1917, two months after his marriage.[28] James began his training in the gloomy and rainy weather of the Pacific Northwest which was different from his new-found home in California.

On the fields of the rainy and gloomy grounds of Camp Lewis, the men of the 91st Division were faced with an expediated training schedule. As Wilson and Tooze explain, the daily drill schedule was packed from 5:45 am to 5:00 pm in the evening.

> First Call was sounded at five-forty-five in the morning, Reveille at six o'clock, with breakfast immediately following inspection between seven and seven-thirty, physical exercise between seven-thirty and eight-thirty, and drill until eleven-thirty. In the afternoon drill began at one and continued until four-thirty when Recall sounded, summoning the troops back to barracks to stand Retreat. Mess was served at five or five-thirty, depending upon the season, and Noncommissioned Officers' School immediately afterward.[29]

---

[27] Spickelmier, "Training of the American Soldier During World War I and World War II," 22.

[28] Ancestry.com. U.S., DEPARTMENT OF VETERANS AFFAIRS BIRLS DEATH FILE, 1850-2010 [database on-line]. Provo, UT, USA: Ancestry.com Operations, Inc., 2011.

[29] Wilson and Tooze. With the 364th Infantry in America, France and Belgium, 5.

As the threat of an impending war was looming over the heads of the 91st Division, the hardline regimen of the military kicked into gear. No longer were the men oil drillers, tailors, farmers, butchers, or steel workers, they were now property of the United States Army and were tasked to fight with the Allied forces. Men that were drafted away from their families and placed in a position to help fight for their country and the mission of democracy in Europe.

*Figure 2.* James A. Bowman at Camp Lewis, Washington, 1918.

After completing the preparation of basic training, it was time for James to leave Camp Lewis and head towards the fighting on the Western Front. The diary begins on a summer evening.

*Wed P.M. June 26th – 18*
*Entrained Camp Lewis at five minutes past four. Train pulled out at 4:30 PM. Going south.*[30]

The 364th Infantry began their fateful trip to the Western Front and James, the shy and reserved man, begins writing his diary with three short sentences. The last time James was on a train making a life-changing journey he was headed out to California for opportunity in the oil industry. This trip, however, was much different than the one made of years before. The diary has only one entry for the day which captures the nerves and anxiety of soldiers shipping out to war. The busy and hectic day of moving out from Camp Lewis wore down the energy level of most men as the uncertainty of a distant war came ever closer with the grinding of the train wheels. The absence of words and short sentences portray a potential anxiety and chaotic time for my great-grandfather to sit and write about his thoughts. With all the uncertainty building up from

[30] All Italicized entries come from the diary of James Austin Bowman unless noted otherwise. Entries are translated verbatim with all spelling and grammar mistakes. James A. Bowman. *Diary, 1918-1919* Transcribed by Cheryl Foy and Alexander Foy.

the day, writing about his experience leaving the Camp was secondary, and rightfully so.

Tooze and Wilson offer another outlook on the departure for war,

> In our hearts we knew we would soon be realizing out great goal, for the need for troops to turn the tide of battle would sooner or later lead to a call for the Ninety-first or 'Wild West' Division and we would go forth from our Alma Mater of military training to lend aid to make the world safe for democracy.[31]

James recounts later in the diary a similar message of protecting democracy abroad and ending the war. It is a unique feature of Wilson and Tooze's account that they hold a different nostalgic viewpoint for their fighting in the Western Front, especially remembering the day when that they had to ship out to fight.

In the next two weeks, James traveled across the United States and into the Midwest, finally ending up in New York. James writes about his journey in the following passages of the diary.

*June 27th 2 P.M.*
*Just passed thru Baker Oregon. Looks like were bound thru Cheyenne, Wym. Stopped at La Grande for exercise and a few moments Liberty. Have passed thru some very beautiful country. The next large town is Chey "shy ann". Slept nice and warm last night but the berth was too short. My bunkie slept like a log and didn't*

---

[31] Bryant Wilson and Lamar Tooze. With the 364th Infantry in America, France and Belgium., 10.

*bother me much except he took up room that I would like to have called my own.*

*June 27th 7:05 P.M.*
*Just crossed into Idaho. We stopped 20 minutes in Huntington Ore. And had the freedom of the town, small town and old fashioned. This part of the country is pretty by spots and in lots of places it looks like the old sage brush hills above Fellows. There was an orphan of little lots played for us in Huntington and we tossed them a few coins they were poor kids. I gave a dime. Brass band.*

*June 28-18 10:10 A.M.*
*Been traveling in Wym for about an hour. Train stopped a few moments in Glen Falls, Idaho, last night at 11 o'clock. There was a large crowd to meet us. The ladies of Red Cross gave us post cards, cigarettes, lemonade, chewing gum etc. The people thru here are very patriotic and meet trains at all hours. We pulled into Pocatello, Idaho at 5:00 oclock this morning. We were all asleep and the girls came along the windows and woke us up. We chewed the rag in our underclothes. Ha. Some trip, but tiresome. Last evening one of our corporals put a shell in his rifle and shot at a Jack Rabbit. He was put under arrest and will be kept there till we reach our port in east. He sure lost his head. We all carry 10 rounds of ammunition. I miss someone very much but she understands that I can't write about it here as some other eyes may read it.*

*June 28-4:10*
*Still drifting thru Wyo waste, just thru Rock Springs, which isn't a bad looking town for Wys. Passed thru Kemmerer where Sam used to work. We are now going over the same road that Sam and I traveled east on in 1915. They marched us all over to the River at Green River to take a swim but there was so much mud we couldn't do it. So we marched back in disgust.*

*June 29 8 A.M.*
*Been in Neb since daylight. Went thru Laramie at midnight; a big crowd. Went thru Chey at 2 A.M. I didn't' look out was too sleepy. Country is green moss. Weather comfortable and cloudy. 11:40 A.M stopped in North Platte after breakfast and look thru town. Everything is going fine.*

*June 30th 6:30 A.M.*
*Nothing much happened between North Platte and Omaha. At Omaha we had about two hours they marched us over town unarmed just for exercise. The Red Cross Ladies gave us little knick knacks. The train stopped in the yards at Council Bluffs quite a crowd gathered. Locomotives whistled factory whistles and hell was a popping. We will soon be in Old Chicago. This trying hard train.*

*7:45 pm*
*Arrive in old Chi little past noon. Marched under arms to the Y.M.C.A. and all took showers. Was in town two hours or more but had no Liberties. The Red Cross gave us cigr & a sandwich. Are somewhere near South Bend now so they say. Traveling on thru Wabash. The bunch is making plenty of noise.*

*July 1st 18- 10:50 A.M.*
*Crossed into Canada at Windsor last night. Natives welcome us at trains. Weather is cool. Dominion Day*

*7:25 P.M.*
*We are back in the U.S.A. crossed at Niagara Falls. We marched unarmed from the American side to the falls. They are a wonderful sight and much larger than I had supposed. The people don't seem to be so friendly here as the Middle West.*

*July 2-18 9:20 A.M.*
*Just crossed into N.J. we travelled awhile in Peoria, woke up this morning to find myself in my old native state, Passed thru Bethlehem, Allentown and Center. Whistle blew and humans chased we are almost there arrived at Dumont at about 2 P.M. Marched a mile to Camp Merritt. I was issued a mattress & cover and two pairs of wrap leggings immediately.*

*July 3-12:45 P.M.*
*Stood reveille as usual this morning, went for a little exercise walk at 8 am had presentation and then drilled till noon. I didn't' eat any dinner today the change of water has made me sort of sick at stomach and don't need physic either.*

*July 4th 2:05 P.M.*
*Just laying around today, turning in unserviceable stuff, washing, writing and trying to feel good feel better than I did yesterday.*

*July 5 -18*
*Still laying around waiting on clothes, signed payroll last night. Haven't all my clothes yet. It is pretty sultry today. I feel better and ate some dinner. The corporal that fired the shot at the Jack Rabbit didn't' get anything done to him. He is still a corporal, was denied, the privilege of leaving the car for a couple of days.*

*July 6th*
*Had Physical drill in morning. Marched to Liberty Theater saw film performed by War Draft "Fit to Fight. Heard a grand sermon by some black suited fellow. We had freedom of camp in evening, went to Y.M.C.A. Audit and had a sing fest and saw a good picture.*

*July 7 Sun.*
*Just hanging around waiting for clothes can't leave barrack ground. No mail yet.*

The only adventure outside of Pennsylvania that James had made in his lifetime was to California with his brother three years earlier. But soon enough, in a few short years after making California his home, James was headed back to the East coast to complete another job; this time, he did not have a choice. As the train moved East, James had stopped off in various cities in the United States. In the long, drawn out road trip, some of the smallest events in Nowhere, U.S.A. had made it onto the pages of James's diary. One notable passage from the trip was when James wrote about a corporal who "put a shell in his rifle and shot at a Jack

Rabbit. He was put under arrest and will be kept there till we reach our port in east."[32] It could have been a variety of reasons why the corporal had shot at the rabbit, maybe from the sheer boredom of the trip, the anxiety of going to war, or maybe just simply he wanted to go hunting. In the journey to New York, it had lasted fifteen days with the infantry drilling during certain stops, it is not a shock that soldiers became more anxious during the journey to the Western Front.

During the passage to New York, the long train ride offered time of reflection particularly for thinking about the love of his life. At the very beginning of the journey, James writes about Evelyn, "I miss someone very much but she understands that I can't write about it here as some other eyes may read it (June 28-18 10:10 AM)."[33] The daily and monthly grind of drilling to maximum level while preparing for the war began to take its toll on James. The unescapable war was right before his very eyes and the only escape was to write to Evelyn. The absence of my great-grandfather's feeling on paper towards my great-grandmother in the early part of

---

[32] James A. Bowman. *Diary, 1918-1919*. Transcribed by Cheryl Foy and Alexander Foy.

[33] James A. Bowman. *Diary, 1918-1919*. Transcribed by Cheryl Foy and Alexander Foy.

the diary show the inability to write about his true feelings in fear of wondering eyes from military post officers and his bunk mates. The privacy that James wanted was unavailable to him because of his shy and reserved nature and as to not attract unwanted attention. My grandfather describes James as the type of man at a dinner party that would be in the back of the room and you would never notice that he was there.[34] The shy personality of James unfolded on paper with the censoring of his thoughts and emotions that he most deeply wanted to express to Evelyn. But as the journey dragged on and as we will see in the next chapter, James will no longer hold back his emotions in the face of an impending war. War brings uncertainty, and the thought of an untimely death raises many questions on why James remained silent in his writings. What if he never got the opportunity to say what he truly wanted to my great-grandmother? Why did he hold back when his safe return home was not guaranteed? One can wonder in war, there are thousands of missed opportunities by those that have died in battle who never felt of the opportunity to say what they wanted in fear of worry from wandering eyes.

---

[34] Robert Bowman, interview by Alexander Foy, February 2017.

Even in the Civil War, a war fought on United States soil, soldiers felt a sense of homesickness and the longing to finish the fight and head home. One Civil War soldier, George Cram, remarked that "the boys are as a general thing terribly homesick and talk of nothing but home, home. Many of them lay in their tents and brood over it."[35] For a soldier traveling further and further away from his home, the weight of the war in an unknown environment becomes a great burden to bear.

On July 12, 1918, James sailed from New York on the ship, R.M.S. Olympic that was headed to South Hampton Harbor in England. The long Atlantic passage did not run as smoothly as luxurious cruise lines that make this same trip today.

> *Had a very disagreeable trip, poor grub and poor sleeping facilities. Was on sentry duty during the entire trip. Was convoyed a day and half out of N.Y. by two airplanes and one U.S. destroyer. Crossed the ocean without convoy met two days off England by 5 U.S. destroyers that convoyed us to the entrance of South Hampton Harbor England. The Olympic carries 6 -6" guns 4 ford and 2 aft. We kept a vigilant watch at all times but no subs appeared. Was met a day or so off England by 2 seaplanes also. We docked at South Hampton out 8 P.M. July 19 and landed the next morning about 9 A.M. Had to hang on the deck all day. Left under the good old stars & stripes that evening about 8 P.M. for Havre France. We docked there about 6 A.M. and landed shortly after raids*

---

[35] George F. Cram to his Mother, January 1, 1863, *Soldiering with Sherman: Civil War Letters of George F. Cram*, ed. Jennifer Cain Bohrnstedt (DeKalb, IL, 2000), 35-36.

*and marched miles to a tent camp that belongs to England. We landed in Havre July 21, Sunday. We leave this camp for the front about 4P.M.*

The Atlantic passage was the prelude to the awaiting hardship that faced the 91st Division and the rest of the US Army. The disagreeable trip would only become worse before it would get any better. As James Bowman stepped off the boat, it was the first time he had been away from "the stars and stripes" and onto foreign land soil. As a new world traveler, James writes the first initial reactions to seeing England at the time.

*England looks like a play house alongside of the U.S.A. Of course we all think the U.S.A. is the only place now and many of the boys don't hesitate to tell the bloody English what they think of them either. The Olympic flies the English flag and of course we were treated like English Soldiers, we are still on their rations here and are getting pretty hungry too. No water here to wash clothes or bath with. Oh give us the old U.S.A. and home again.*

As James continues to write in the entry, the following passage looks like a letter that was sent to him that he copied into the diary.

*Don't forget that you have a wife and your main duty is to write to her every day or she is liable to get another fellow. Don't eat too many bananas remember your filling and if you do eat them chew each bite five minutes before you swallow it see? Save your money and don't spend it all for candy, remember when you get home? Please think of me just once in a while and remember I will always love you. I will be a*

> *good girl while you are gone and won't go out with any fellow or flirt or even look at a man. I will pray for you every night dearest and I know God will take care of my love and keep him safe for one that loves him better than life. By the time you get home I will have a very large fortune stowed away and then we will buy the little nest we have planned to have so long ago and a little Jimmie that you will have to walk the floor nights with while I am sleeping. Always remember that I love, love, love you and you are always with me in my thoughts from day to day.*

The letter is believed to have come from my great-grandmother, Evelyn. The letter gives clues with the writing about being a loyal wife while he was away and the thought of a little Jimmie to walk the floor nights.[36] This was possibly the first letter he received overseas after being away from Evelyn. I do not have any record of the original copy of the letter, but it contained a significant meaning for my great-grandfather. In the letter, Evelyn writes with a sense of sarcasm that urges James to remain faithful in constantly writing or she will go out to find "another fellow." This letter comes early on in their married relationship and shows a sense of flirting as a working-class woman that is keeping her new husband entertained as he is off to war. The letter is written verbatim in the diary and

---

[36] Little Jimmie would become my great-uncle, James Marshall Bowman, who served in the United States Navy on a PT boat in the Philippines during World War II. Unlike James Austin, little Jimmie did not see any combat while overseas. (Robert Bowman, interview by Alexander Foy, November 2017.)

contains a message of a profound love. The letter is written in a playful manner where it captures the new "puppy dog" love of their relationship. She writes about a future of kids and saving money to start a new life even though there is a chance that James may never return. The diary is considered a private space where one can write their own thoughts, but there is always a chance that it could be read by other soldiers. James knew that this letter could be seen by others which made it a significant piece of his diary that he was not afraid to hide. The letter from Evelyn is open and affectionate which does not bother James if anyone were to read.

While the 91st Division was making its way towards France, the Germans had launched their last offensive on July 15, 1918 in the Second Battle of Marne, located in the Champagne region of France. Erich Ludendorff, the German general, led the campaign to lure the Allied troops away from his primary target which was in Flanders, the region stretching from northern France into Belgium.[37] The Marne River was set as the battle to divert the Allied Powers away from Flanders, in hopes to divide French troops and capture the region. The Battle of the Marne proved that the Allied powers

---

[37] Manufacture de Caoutchouc Michelin. 1917. *Battle of the Marne*. Michelin & Co. http://hdl.handle.net/2027/coo.31924005794411.

could defeat the German troops which turned the tide of the war. Soon the Allied troops would begin their own offensives to push back the German troops from France.

## On the Front

As the war on the Western Front had intensified for the Allied forces in pushing back the German troops, the 364th Infantry began their trek to the frontlines in France. The harsh reality of war began to set in for James and the rest of the Infantry as the advanced form of transportation for these soldiers was their own two feet.

*July 25*
*We are billeted in some small interior town. We traveled 2 nights and two days camped in a little box car with half rations. Was very tired when we detrained and was very much surprised to find we had to take a 15 mile hike to our billets we made it on pure guts alone. We fell to our sleeps at once and was dead for several hours. Haven't had any breakfast yet, it is 11:40 A.M. We were a sight when we arrived last night dirty, unshaven, dead and hungry. Words can't express it.*

As soon as the Infantry made it close to the front, the traveling was over for these men. After an absence of hard training, the leaders of the division began training the Infantry with a sense of urgency in order to prepare them for combat. With each passing day, the reality of battle became not just a thought but a reality.

*Aug 4th 18*

*Haven't been paying much attention to my little diary lately. Well there isn't a great deal of excitement to write about. We are drilling hard all the time and what little time we have to ourselves we have to keep clean shave, and talk about good old America, those good days we spent over there and didn't know what fortunate mortals we were. I know I've lost weight, we all have, our eat are very scant and I've been without any money to buy with. I have six francs now and will take good care of it.*

*They are drilling us too hard. We are all tired out and absolutely lifeless. We work so hard we can't put anything into our work. I was on Military Police Duty for several days, but they changed the guard to the way we did it at Camp Lewis there are six companies here F, G, H, I. R. and the Machine Gun Co. So we will get guard every six days.*

*We see airplanes fly over most every day and can hear the big guns once in a while. We don't get much war news but all we have gotten so far is to our credit. We are all crazy to get to the front and have it over with. I am feeling more and more that the war is nearly over but I believe our little Company will see fighting and they are going to give an account of themselves. We have some good news in Co. F. We are billeted in Millieres France. We got our first mail today, but there was none for me as usual and very badly disappointed.*

*Aug 15th 18*
*One year ago yesterday was married to the best and dearest girl that ever breathed. God bless her. Am resting at present in the shade of some small trees near a stream of water somewhere in France. Have just had lunch and an ice cold bath. Feeling fine so much for that. Have had very little time to myself, haven't written any letters and just can't help it.*

James recalls his anniversary, not with a warm cooked dinner at home or a picnic with his wife, instead in two short sentences. Two sentences are all that James can write to his internal monologue because the place he wants to be is thousands of miles away.

Anniversaries in American culture are a celebration, where a couple could reflect on where they have been and what the future lies ahead. James was only able to reflect through his words. One of the important details in the passage regarding his anniversary is the absence of words that James uses to describe the ceremonial event. In the context of the diary, he had gone in a matter of months from upstate Washington to the middle of war-torn France, with each day bringing an unexpected drill or a possible battle. One of the best ways to describe the current moment on August 15, 1918, is chaos. Within a matter of three years, James moved to another state, was married, drafted into the service, and sent to the Western Front to fight in the war. Like many soldiers that entered the war, the son of a small Pennsylvania town, he may have never predicted how his life would turn out in a few short months. But the reality of war is simply that it is unpredictable. In a matter of days, decisions, or moments, your life can be changed forever.

The diary continues August 15, 1918,

*We are ready to leave for the front at 48 hr. Notice we've turned in everything except what we carry on our backs when we leave, but we will be loaded. Will carry our overcoats & slickers too. We've signed the payroll and guess we will get paid soon. Still have 3 francs. I started chewing a little the other day. I don't know why I did it, I didn't crave it but we are worked so hard I just got disgusted and chewing help to pass off the monotony. I know now that I can quit at any time and will do so as soon as things are going better.*

*We wear our steel hats at all drills now. We get lots of drill that seems foolish to me, now just as we are about to go into the battle front we should have more schooling in combat work and such as that. Well we've a good bunch of men and if God is willing we will pull thru in good shape. Will sure be happy to get back to the one little woman and our little home again.*

*Sunday Sept 1-18*
*Have been too busy to write much in the little diary these last two weeks, even at that there haven't been any thing happening of much account. We are not worked so long hours now but we have to pack our full packs everywhere and it is hard work. I can't see the sense in it and if anyone can explain it to me. I wish they would do so. Got #4 letter from Evelyn this A.M. and have begun the answer. We go on a three day Divisional hike tomorrow and get paid Wed afternoon.*

*Sept 3-18 A.M.*
*We've been packed ready to leave since yesterday morning. Didn't go on the Division hike. Everybody is happy and ready for the fray. The boys had to throw stuff away they couldn't take along and these natives fared well. They are all better fixed financially too as the bulk of our pay is left in the town. They are money grabbers. We expect to fall out this P.M. but no one knows were waiting orders.*

*Sept 4*
*They fooled us once yesterday called us out in marching orders. Marched us out of town and turned around and came back. We fill in again about 1 P.M. and then left Millieres for good. We billeted in this town last night. I don't know the name of it. They got the kitchen set up and we had supper about 9:30 P.M. thu we had quite assemble making nest in the hay. I had a good bed and slept fairly will altho got cold towards morning. We carry our ungodly heavy load. I carry 90 rounds rifle ammunition and 35 pistol. We are awaiting orders to leave now 8:50 A.M. I also am carrying the Auto rifle, it weighs about 21 lbs. some of the men are carrying 200 rounds of ammunition. The name of this town is Longue.*

*Sept 5-18 4 P.M.*
*We are still here. Got word that we can send our coats and shoes by truck to the point where we entrain that will lighten our load considerably. Was out at pistol practice this P.M. Read letter from Kitt today. It rained some, enough to lay the dust. We expect to leave tomorrow.*

*Sept 16-18*
*We had an early breakfast one morning and marched to some railroad town (I forgot the name) near Nogent. We camped there one night and entrained the next evening and went to Gondrecourt. Arrived there about 1 A.M. detrained and slept in a field till 8 A.M. had coffee and marched out about five miles and camped in the woods about three days. Marched one night to the wood near Pagny 15 miles and camped there two nights then went into Billets at Pagny for one night. The next evening we packed into trucks and rode all night long to this small town on the Verdun front. We've been here two night and three days now. Could see and the bombardment last night of the French and American on the Verdun sector. Was in Reserved_Pagny where the American started their drive on St Mihiel. They bombarded all night long and it was some noise. In the evening, we are ready to move out sometime tonight. The name of this town is Villette.*

James Bowman and the rest of the 364th Infantry would wait in reserve while the combined American French offensive attempted to end the war for good. The two pieces of the American plan, led by John Pershing, General of the American Expeditionary Forces (A.E.F.), was to attack St. Mihiel and the Meuse Argonne areas to expel the Germans and push them back. The first major engagement for the A.E.F. was the Battle of St. Mihiel, which began on September 12, 1918. The St. Mihiel engagement was over before it began. The region had lost its value to the Germans, but Pershing believed in bringing overwhelming force.[38] The St. Mihiel engagement also shined a light on the disorganization of the United States military in its attempt to get as many trained men to the front. Once the St. Mihiel engagement was over, it turned to a logistical nightmare for the AEF as they began to turn their attention to the Meuse-Argonne region. The transportation system that would plague the effectiveness of the AEF would soon affect the men preparing to fight in the Meuse Argonne Offensive. The men had to transport over 900,000 tons of supplies into the Meuse Argonne sector.[39] As the rain began to sweep into the region, the transportation system was dealt another blow of having to navigate on wet and muddy roads. "Truck transport was not much better than walking . . . the trucks, which had no springs, were excruciatingly uncomfortable, with sixteen men and packs jammed together on the floorboards."[40] James was faced with this disorganized system in his journey to the Meuse-Argonne Offensive.

---

[38] Robert H. Ferrell, *America's Deadliest Battle: Meuse-Argonne, 1918*. (Lawrence, Kansas: University Press of Kansas, 2007.), 32-33.

[39] Ferrell, America's Deadliest Battle: Meuse-Argonne, 1918., 37.

[40] Ferrell, America's Deadliest Battle: Meuse-Argonne, 1918., 37-38.

*Sept 19*
*We left Villette at about 9 P.M. Sept 16 the trucks were supposed to come for us but they never came so we had to hoof it 20 miles that night. Most every man threw away extra shoes, overcoats and other articles. It was the toughest marched I ever had hundreds of men fill out I made it but was all in just able to waddle along. We camped in woods about 5 A.M. I changed underclothes went to sleep and on ground and about 7:30 it began to rain hard. It never woke me till after I was all wet. We pitched our tent but was so wet we couldn't sleep anymore had no drinking water and was in a miserable plight for a while.*

*We march 9 miles that night and am now in an orchard near a small deserted town that the German have almost destroyed. There are no civilians here. We've been here two nights now. I think we will go in the trenches to night. I understand to relieve a French Division. There is almost a continues from bombard here. Last night at sunset a Boche plane hovered over us awhile. We expected to be bombed but were disappointed. The allied anti-aircraft guns kept it out of their range. Later a French plane returning from the front drove it away. The Frenchman had no ammunition. He shot one magazine at the Boche and then beat it. It was quite a sight for all of us. We expected to be in either shelled or bombed last night but nothing happened. The attitude and conduct of our men is practically the same as at Camp Lewis. The fact they we are in the danger zone and are soon to be in action seems to have no effect whatever in fact every one of us are eager to get into the scrap and get it over and get home.*

After the grueling march of twenty-nine miles in two days, James Bowman and the rest of the 364th Infantry inched to the waiting room of the war. The trucks never came to pick up James and transport him the twenty miles it required to make it to the front. With the wet conditions, the route to Meuse Argonne was a disaster in terms of the logistics of transportation. In a few short days and mere miles away from the frontlines, the war was closer to the 364th Infantry than ever before. Gas alarms and German shrapnel put the pressure on James as a constant reminder of what is in store for him as he inches closer to the German frontline.

The sheer willpower and grit it took for the men of the AEF to make the long march to the Meuse Argonne Offensive is nothing short of extraordinary. James was overcome with exhaustion after the march and slept through the downpour of rain. Over the last couple of weeks, James has been writing about the rations and physical toll of drilling in preparation for war. For four months, James had been in reserve, fulfilling his duty with military police in French villages and drilling to prepare for the potential of war. James had been itching to go to war and being so close to the front made it even more of a reality.

In the September 19th entry, James mentions the term "Boche" for the very first time. "Boche" originated from the French soldiers when speaking of the Germans. When the United States soldiers encountered the French, they began to refer to the Germans as the "Boche". "Boche" is an abbreviation of caboche. It is a recognized French word use for head, specially a big, thick head.

"Boche" originated before World War I, around 1870, where Parisian printers applied the term to "their German assistants because of the reputed slowness of comprehension of these foreign printers."[41] The French would use the term "tête de boche" in propaganda posters which translates in French as a slang of blockhead or unintelligent for the Germans.

The march to the Western Front continued. In the next entry, the tone of James starts to change to nervousness as a looming engagement approached.

*Sept 21-18*
*We fell in about 7:p.m. on the 18th left the orchard later on and marched within one mile of the German front. We are now encamped in a wood and are awaiting the big drive. We don't do anything here but hauf under cover and eat two scant meals a day. Last night we had two gas alarms, one was real but the gas didn't reach any of us the last alarm was accidental. Allied planes are over us constantly and draw fire from the Boche anti air guns. Bits of shrapnel fall amongst us some times but so far no one has been hit. I don't think the Boche knows what is going on here. Yet we look for shelling at any time. We are getting a well deserve rest but it would be more to our liking to get more to eat. A French gun near us keeps poking away at the Boche all night long and it is hard to sleep. Anyway it is cold and rains most of the time and it is hard to sleep anyway. Oh! for home and happiness again. This will surely be the deciding drive of the war.*

---

[41] Douglas Buffum, "Origin of the Word 'Boche,'" *Current History: A Monthly Magazine of the New York Times*, Vol. 4 (1916): 525.

The Meuse Argonne Offensive loomed over the men of the 364th Infantry like a ghost. On September 25, the US Army ordered that "no American allow himself to be taken prisoner; that it would be one's duty to take one's life rather than to be taken prisoner."[42] The order was bound by secrecy from the men in the infantry and not spoken of by many for the rest of their lives. Another part of the war that my great-grandfather never shared in the diary and took to his grave.

After months of training and drilling, the soldiers of the 91st Division have been waiting for this moment to take advantage by using their weapons and the skills that they have gained over the last couple of months. I could not imagine getting into the psyche of my great-grandfather on the eve of battle, knowing that you will have to fire your rifle towards another living human. The thought makes my stomach turn. My great-grandfather probably did not get much sleep that night before battle. In all the instances throughout the diary, my great-grandfather was eager to go to battle and get into the fray. He had constant drilling that pushed his body to the limit in order to prepare him physically for the physical toll of war. The men of the

---

[42] Bryant Wilson and Lamar Tooze. With the 364th Infantry in America, France and Belgium., 49.

91st Division had a craving for battle after the months of mundane training and marching. It was not a craving for blood, instead they wanted to get the war over and get home to the "good ole USA." For my great-grandfather, the eagerness for battle was primarily focused on getting the job done and getting out as soon as possible. Months and months of training came to a point where men were *wanting* for an engagement in battle and their wish came true. The 364th Infantry had been on the Western Front for two months until the order came from the US Army came on September 25. It was going to be the largest engagement of the war. James writes in the diary on the eve of the Meuse Argonne Offensive.

*Sept 25-18*
*We are packed ready for the battle. We leave the woods sometime today and I guess the Artillery will offer up tonight or maybe this P.M. The Bokeh did quite a lot of bombarding last night but none in our area. We had one gas alarm. Everyone is tickled to death to be off and our turned up to the proper pitch for the fray. It is going to be a great move, the biggest of the war and it is bound to be a success. We had a late, but good breakfast and are starting out with plenty of ammunition and reserve rations. Look out Boche.*

## September 26, 1918

The front lines of the battlefield stretched nearly eighteen miles from the Argonne Forest in the west to the Meuse River in the east. The terrain of the battlefield was mostly "hilly and broken, and a large part of it is heavily wooded."[43] The lines that divided the Allied forces and the Germans had remained stationary and stagnant for three years. The Germans had used the Meuse Argonne Offensive as a staging area for the Verdun attack in 1916 so they had "constructed fortifications and artillery shelters throughout the sector."[44] With the German army sustaining losses from the two-front war, Erich Ludendorff issued a reinforcement of these fortifications along the front in order to stop the Allied advancements. The issue of reinforcement became known as the Hindenburg Line. The Hindenburg Line was the "German fortified line of defense on the Western Front to which Field Marshal Paul von Hindenburg directed retreat."[45] The line was a triple-lined entrenched position, with barbed wire and concrete pillboxes with machine guns which extended north to south along the eastern border of France.[46] It had soon become an objective for the Allied

---

[43] 91st Division Publication Committee. *The Story of the 91st Division*. (San Mateo, CA: H. S. Crocker Co, Inc., 1919), 10.

[44] Richard Shawn Faulkner. *Meuse-Argonne 26 September-11 November 1918*. U.S. Army Campaigns of World War I. 2018, 12.

[45] "Hindenburg Line." *The Oxford Essential Dictionary of the U.S. Military*, 2001, The Oxford Essential Dictionary of the U.S. Military.

[46] "Hindenburg Line." *The Oxford Essential Dictionary of the U.S. Military*, 2001, The Oxford Essential Dictionary of the U.S. Military.

forces to finally make ground in the stagnant war. With a reinforced trench defense and the dense landscape of the Argonne Forest, it offered great protection for the German army and a large challenge for the mobility for the United States Army. The American Expeditionary Force's only major combat fighting was with the St. Mihiel (September 12-16), so the Meuse Argonne Offensive was going to be its largest test.[47]

At 2:30 am in the morning, A.E.F. and French artillery began a barrage of firepower that aimed to take out the barbed wire and other field fortifications. With the barbed wire and field fortifications neutralized, it would give American infantry an easier fighting terrain. The artillery would continue its barrage for nearly three hours. After the artillery ceased firing, the moment came for the United States troops spread out across the frontlines.

At 5:30 am, the call came out from the American commanders to storm out of the trenches towards the various German positions in these hilly, broken fields of the French forest. It was September 26, 1918 and on this fateful day, the Meuse-Argonne Offensive had begun.

---

[47] Ferrell, America's Deadliest Battle: Meuse-Argonne, 1918., 27.

As the mist clouds your vision you continue to look forward. A deafening noise crashes with every blast all around you. With every loud boom comes the spray of dirt. It is chaos. For the months of training, it seems like no one knows what to do. Officers yelling orders. It's no use because the guns are deafening. Your rifle is loaded with ammo. Bullets. A metal cylinder filled with gun powder. One of these can end a life of my enemy. One of these can end my own life. A deep breath. You rise from the trench and take my first shot. It was blind. You don't know if it hit anything or anyone. What if it hit flesh? Machine gun fire and a grenade blast. You can't think. It's too loud. Your officers yell orders but how can we follow them when there is so much chaos around us. It begins. The shrieks of terror. Men lying cold on the ground. A life ended in a matter of a second.

It begins. The screams. Oh, the screams. The screams of your fellow soldiers yelling as they take their last breath. Crying out to the world that created their existence. And that same world that was ending it. Sitting with your back against the dirt wall that divided you from constant fire and you're useless to those men. You can't aid them or cure their wounds because the carnage was too deep.

Your thoughts are racing through your mind. More machine gun fire and grenade blasts continue. You react with primal instinct. The months of training for a war, you were drafted into, have all come to this moment. Like an actor in the theater or an athlete in a championship game, months of preparation are for this one moment. You grasp your rifle even tighter. Your heart is beating so fast, you wonder how it hasn't fallen out of your chest yet. More machine gun fire and a grenade blast. This time the shattered dirt exploded closer to your location. You can't go home now. You're thousands of miles away. Away from Pennsylvania, where your father and stepmother sit at their kitchen table. Away from the oil drills, where you would trade the worst and most miserable day on the job, for this very moment. Away from Fellows, California, your new home. Away from Evelyn, your love. Away from Evelyn, waiting all alone for news of the war. Dreading the moment, the newspaper comes, or the mail gets delivered, "Mrs. Bowman." The two words she was striving to avoid in any letter postmarked from the US Army. She sits alone. Countless nights, where each day seems like a nightmare since she received word of your deployment to France. Fear creeps into her mind. What if I become a widow? Machine gun fire and a grenade blast. This time you hear the engine of the plane roar. It's only 7:30 am. You've been at this for only an hour, yet it seems like an eternity. This is war. This is your life. No longer are you in the safe presence of small-town Sandy Lake. No time to waste because the moment you stop to think, you're dead. Evelyn. One step closer to Evelyn. So, you gulp down spit and receive a hint of tobacco and rise from behind the dirt wall, you fire in the direction of your enemy. Back down in behind the wall. You stop to realize what happened. You look over your shoulder to the land in front of you. You peer through the valley of hell. "No Man's Land." they call it. It is hell and nothing survives there. And in a few short moments, you are going to run across this forest of hell.

The day began with misty and smoky air that clouded the battlefield. By mid-noon, the mist had faded with the sun shining on the Meuse Argonne Offensive allowing for a rare moment that would soon be filled with rain, mud, and destruction. As the other divisions and infantries began their assault early in the morning, the 364$^{th}$ Infantry had a unique route to finding lanes of wires between Mont des Aillieux and La Cigarlerie. The Infantry had reached the jumping off point around 6:30 am, one hour after the initial hour of reckoning. By 7:00 am, the 364th Infantry was nearly 500 meters behind the 363rd Infantry but had navigated across No-Man's Land with the 1st Battalion having success. The 2nd Battalion did not have the same luck. When the 2nd Battalion, headquarter, and machine gun companies reached the valley of the Buanthe, they were soon met with machine gun fire from the northern slope of Vauquois Hill.[48] Brigadier General Frederick S. Foltz, 182nd infantry brigade (the brigade that involved the 364th Infantry), instilled an offensive tactic very much different to General Pershing's vision for the offensive. Foltz instituted a tactic of moving forward in a column which only used one battalion at a time, rather than using all six battalions.[49] The mistake by Foltz was quickly corrected after a colonel had replaced him to carry carried out Pershing's vision of the Offensive.

As the second day of the Offensive on September 27, the 364th Infantry was met with hostile shelling from the Germans right before they were to begin their assault. The 364th Infantry moved towards the town of Eclisfontaine and captured the town around 4:30

---

[48] 91st Division Publication Committee. *The Story of the 91st Division.*, 24.

[49] Ferrell, Robert H. America's Deadliest Battle: Meuse-Argonne, 1918, 47.

pm after help from the artillery. The Meuse Argonne Offensive was coming together for the American Expeditionary Force as they were able to push back the German forces and establish a line running through Epinonville, Eclisfontaine, and Les Bouleaux Bois.[50]

The first two days required great determination, grit, and work to gain tremendous ground on the Germans, but the third day required more fighting to deplete the Germans strongholds. On the third day, September 28, the 364th Infantry began its push to the frontline to overtake the German resistance at Eclisfontaine, Varennes road, Serieux Farms, and Les Bouleaux Bois. The heavy machine gun nests pounded the infantry, but soon the Infantry were able to take positions on the road, farm, and woods by noon of that day. The pushes by the various infantries within the 91st Division exposed them to attacks from the west.[51] But once the infantries were able to make contact, they were able to fortify the line. During the early days of fighting, one tactic used by the men during the Offensive was to create spacing between the soldiers in order to avoid causalities from the artillery barrages. Awaiting the Allied

---

[50] 91st Division Publication Committee. *The Story of the 91st Division*, 30.

[51] 91st Division Publication Committee. *The Story of the 91st Division*, 31.

forces in the Argonne Forest were numerous traps from the Germans. Grenades had been placed in buildings and connected with wire, which meant opening the door would set off the explosion. Mines were buried along trails and tramways.[52] A fellow soldier in the 91st Division, Vernon Nichols, "remembered his platoon being spread out according to specialty . . . and when work was to be done, a group double-timed up forming a skirmish line with spacing as wide as fifteen yards."[53]

The fourth day marked an even tougher day for the 91st Division. Late at night, the Corps Commander directed a renewal of the attack starting at 7:00 am the next day. As the 91st Division book remarks, the division "obeyed this order on that memorable Sunday with renewed energy and inspiration, believing each division would be prompted by the same impulse to 'do or die' for the Fifth Corps."[54] The 91st Division had been assigned the important task of "carrying the ball through the center of the First American Army."[55]

---

[52] Wilson and Tooze, With the 364th Infantry in American, France, and Belgium., 62.

[53] Nichols, Vernon. "Our Battle of the Argonne." Infantry Journal no. 16 (September 1919): 188.

[54] 91st Division Publication Committee. *The Story of the 91st Division*, 32.

[55] 91st Division Publication Committee. *The Story of the 91st Division*, 32.

James had been fighting with relatively no sleep or rest for nearly 72 hours. The only rest he would get during the breaks in the fighting must have been minimal compared to the energy needed to fight for your life.

By September 30, the 91st Division had dug in a fortified defensive position south of Exmorieux Farm and north of the recently captured Eclisfontaine highway. The 91st Division had covered a significant amount of land in the last four days. Protecting the defensive line was no easy task as leftover German snipers randomly attacked the Allied forces. The snipers were concealed in the woods and proved to be a problem for the Allied forces as they tried to administer aid to the wounded. The German snipers had escalated their level of stealth by concealing their identity by putting on articles of the American uniform which they had picked up on the battlefield.[56] Members of the 91st Division had hunted down many of these snipers and displayed bravery in the face of point-blank fire that helped to eliminate this threat.

On October 1 and 2, the same defensive posture inaction continued for the 91st Division. The Division had continued to hold

---

[56] Wilson and Tooze. With the 364th Infantry in America, France and Belgium, 80.

the line, digging deeper trenches, and "waiting for something to develop."[57] As the sun rose on October 3rd, it marked the eighth day on the line for the men of the 364th Infantry. The men had been advancing for three days and waiting for the last five days. As Wilson and Tooze remark, "it was waiting that was the real test. We had been in the fight for over a week living on cold bully beef and hard-tack; we were sick with dysentery; we had endured eight nights without blanket or overcoats; our nerves had been sorely tired by the loss of sleep and the strain of battle."[58] But on October 3, the artillery barrage began from the German military. Wilson and Tooze describe it as "the most intense artillery fire of the whole engagement."[59] It was shell after shell thrown at the positions of the men until eight o'clock that night. On October 4, the men of the 91st Division were relieved by the 32nd Division and the 1st Division. The Germans continued their artillery barrage as the men marched back across the hills and valleys of what was captured a week earlier.[60]

---

[57] Wilson and Tooze. With the 364th Infantry in America, France and Belgium, 80.

[58] Wilson and Tooze. With the 364th Infantry in America, France and Belgium, 84.

[59] Wilson and Tooze. With the 364th Infantry in America, France and Belgium, 84-85.

[60] Douglas Mastriano, *Thunder in the Argonne: A New History of America's Greatest Battle*, (Kentucky: University Press of Kentucky, 2018), 169.

The men continued to march away from the Front through the towns of Dombasle and the new billeting headquarters, Bussy-la-Côte. By the time the Infantry had received word of their next destination, James was admitted to the base hospital for dysentery, one of the most common diseases on the Western Front.

One of the most important features of the Meuse Argonne Offensive, especially when it comes to the experience of the 91st Division, was the German use of machine gun nests. The 91st Division describes the machine gun nest as "the backbone of the Boche defense."[61] The German machine gun nests would "consist of one or several guns, sometimes set in prepared emplacements, sometimes merely tucked away in bushes or in ruins of a house."[62] When the A.E.F. was held up by machine gun nests, they were unable to advance until the nest has been taken out or by maneuvering around it. When maneuvering around the machine gun nests, they would eventually be met with fire from a different nest which would cause a major standstill within the line until these forces could be taken out. A machine gun nest could be "either

---

[61] 91st Division Publication Committee. *The Story of the 91st Division*, 25.

[62] 91st Division Publication Committee. *The Story of the 91st Division*, 25.

shelled out or held under our own infantry and machine gun fire until they can be stalked by little groups of determined men."[63] Machine gun nests made up much of the terror that was inflicted on the men fighting in the Meuse Argonne Offensive. The only story that my grandfather, Robert, remembers James Bowman sharing from his time during the war was that he and a group of other soldiers stormed up a hill to take over a machine gun nest. This story contained great significance as we will see later in the story of James Bowman.

*Oct 14-18*
*Well the drive is over and I am safe. Am in a base hospital somewhere in France with Dysentery. I wasn't able to march with the Regiment so they sent me here to recuperate. Am getting along fine. Of the drive I will say very little. Words cannot describe it and any attempt on my part might spoil the picture in my memory that I can never forget. We started over the stop at dawn Sept 26 and was under constant fire and all sorts of hardships for nine days when we were relieved by the First Division. Bully Beef and exposure was the course of my sickness. We hear today that Germany has strafed Wilson's planes so we are in good spirits and pray to God to let us go home soon.*

---

[63] 91st Division Publication Committee. *The Story of the 91st Division*, 25.

*Figure 3.* 91st Division at the Meuse Argonne Offensive[64]

Eighteen days later, James recounts in written form for the very first time what he saw on the battlefield. James was resting in a

---

[64] American Battle Monuments Commission, *1st division, summary of operations in the World War.* Washington, D.C.: U.S. Government Printing Office, 1944.

base hospital with dysentery, which is an extreme form of diarrhea. Most Allied forces were placed on rations of "bully beef" which was canned corned beef. The soldiers had seen the French words bouilli boeuf, which means boiled beef, on the cans.[65] Exposure to the wet and muddy conditions opened James to the possibility of contracting a virus or infection. Laying in a base hospital far from the frontlines this very well could have been the first time James was ever able to reflect fully the magnitude what just happened on the front. In one short paragraph, James deconstructs in so few words what he saw. "Of the drive I will say very little. Words cannot describe it and any attempt on my part might spoil the picture in my memory that I can never forget."[66] Words have been attempted to describe, justify, and critique war from historians, politicians, and civilians. But for those that have experienced combat, words cannot describe the terror, atrocities and terrible acts that evolve and devolve on the battlefield. My great-grandfather could not describe the events of the Offensive because any attempt would haunt his ability to cope with the loss of life and the fresh blood that was spilled on the battlefield.

---

[65] Sylvia Lovegren, "Bully Beef." *The Oxford Encyclopedia of Food and Drink in America*, 2004, The Oxford Encyclopedia of Food and Drink in America.

[66] James A. Bowman. *Diary, 1918-1919.* Transcribed by Cheryl Foy and Alexander Foy.

James experienced before his very eyes, the worst of human beings and the evil of war. The act of taking another life has been a test to the morality of humankind since the creation of our existence. The inner historian in me is fascinated with this gap in the description of the battle but instead of focusing on the words that James does not say, James gives us the reality of war. When James describes these memories that he can never forget and the absences of words, it gives the reader an empty feeling of what transpired on the battlefield. In the World War I memoir, *Toward the Flame*, Hervey Allen described his experience being shelled by artillery during the war. Allen described the shelling as "the worst thing in the world. It is impossible to imagine it adequately."[67] Allen goes into further detail in describing the feeling and experience as the shells rain down.

> There is a faraway moan that grows to a scream, then a roar like a train, followed by a ground-shaking smash and a diabolical red light. In the valley the echoes were tremendous. About eleven o'clock the range shifted and shell after shell fell directly among the men – the most awful screams and moans – cries for stretchers from "C" company. We couldn't find where they were in the dark.[68]

---

[67] Hervey Allen. 1926. *Toward the Flame*. New York: George H. Doran Co.43.

[68] Allen, *Toward the Flame*., 43-44.

Allen had a similar experience to James in trying to cope with war through the act of writing. Like James, Allen could not comprehend the ways to retell the story of what happened when the shells fell. It is a feeling of loss and despair. The inability to cope with seeing bodies drop and cries scream out for the last time. The screams become too powerful and the images become too real to ever forget, let alone to construct meaning in written word. These two accounts from Allen and James describe the effect of war as giving them no choice but to move on from the traumatic events. As Nigel Hunt, explains in the book *Memory, War, and Trauma*, coping during war can have different justifications for soldiers like avoidance, fatalism, or no choice. From the accounts by Allen and James, it could be perceived that they both had a mentality of avoidance when coping with their experience in war. Hunt describes avoidance as "soldiers were trained to respond automatically to particular situations, to avoid thinking about the potential personal consequences of their – or their enemy's – actions."[69] For these

---

[69] Nigel C. Hunt, *Memory, War and Trauma.* Leiden: Cambridge University Press, 2010, 149.

soldiers, even after the battle, there was no time or desire to think about the death of your comrades or the enemies.[70]

James is not the only soldier of the Meuse Argonne Offensive to express a sense of shock and disgust. A soldier in the 315th Infantry remarked that the events of September 28, 1918 at the Meuse Argonne Offensive "can never be erased from the minds of the men who were there; words can never describe it, nor is the mind imaginative enough to conceive it."[71] The events that unleashed itself on the Meuse Argonne Offensive is indescribable for any historian to measure the atrocities and destruction on the fields of France. Sergeant Edward Davies reflected in his diary as he was sitting in a shell hole with mud up to his waist.

> The Germans started to shell our position, God it was awful. Saw a man blown to pieces just below where Monty and I were lying . . . I am sick and disgusted with this life. It seems to me that the men who are killed are better off. This is simply a living death, Hell can hold no terrors for me after this. We are not men any more, just savage beasts. There is no fear in me now I would go forward willingly and play the game. If I come thru I am thankful, if not – well its simply part of the game.[72]

---

[70] Hunt, Memory, War and Trauma., 149.

[71] United States Army. 315th Infantry. The official history of the 315th Infantry U. S. A.; being a true record of its organization and training, of its operations in the World War, and of its activities following the signing of the armistice. -1919. [Philadelphia, 1920] Web. https://lccn.loc.gov/20021501, 157.

[72] Sergeant Edward A. Davies, 79th Division, 315 Regiment, WWIS, MHI.

Meuse Argonne was hell. For the men fighting in the Argonne Forest of France, it seemed as if they were on another planet where the rules of man did not apply. War tested, not only the values of James Bowman, but the values of countless other men that had to endure the constant barrage of artillery fire and attacks from the Germans. The accounts of war vary in variety from James Bowman's recollection to the vivid description of Edward Davies. It is a unique perspective to place the experience of James Bowman with other men of the A.E.F. because it enlightens the chaotic nature of war that purges the very soul of the men that fight within the confines of the trenches.

Besides the story of capturing the machine gun nest, this account of the war is the only information James gives on the Meuse Argonne Offensive. The next entry expands some more on the impact of the Meuse Argonne Offensive after James is given time to recoup from his dysentery.

*Oct 15-18*
*Am feeling quite a heap better today, had an examination today, the Dr said I could have my clothes so guess I can get up tomorrow and get cleaned up. Had a big dinner today and it never left any bad effects. Wrote part of a letter to Evelyn, but had no paper to finish it. The prospects of an early peace was on our minds yesterday but have vanished today. However the end is near and the world knows*

*it. My bet we will be a happy bunch when we know we can soon return to that dear old land of freedom. My children shall be taught Patriotisms as a sort of religion as long as the stars and stripes continue to wave in the just and righteous cause it now stands for. It has never been stained with dishonor and man be unto the man that dares to degrade it. The Army to a man stands back of it and President Wilson. I can't help but dream of the good I have derived so far out of this conflict. It has opened my eyes to possibilities of a richer life and a faith that shall linger on thru the years and with the Love of a woman so noble and pure such as I guess I know I shall be fully repaid for all these hardships and privations I've been thru. Looking back over the years I can't understand how I was ever so blind as to make so many mistakes and get so little out of life when all the time I was surrounded with all these riches. However it is done and must be forgotten. It is to you Evelyn that I owe all these riches you showed me the open door and helped me in. I owe a debt to you I can never fully repay but by jinks. I'll keep at it and if love will ever pay the bill I can pay quite a heap of it in time.*

James begins to open on a deeper level about the impact of war. With the knowledge of his shy nature, everything that James writes about in the past two passages is revealing. In every diary or letter, there is bound to be some silences but what James puts down in pencil helps give us a deeper look into how he was coping with the Meuse Argonne Offensive. The tone of the diary begins to change. James is no longer a soldier idly waiting for war to start, instead, he is a soldier who has seen the atrocities of war unfold before his eyes. He had only heard stories or read passages in the paper that described what happened in the war. This time he had experienced it firsthand. James, who is usually reserved in his writing, begins to discuss his feeling with his sacred space of the diary. The diary serves as a portal where James could begin to process the events of the Meuse Argonne Offensive. The last two diary entries were written nearly two weeks after the Offensive began so James has had time to decompress and process what transpired in the Argonne Forest. The entry of October 15 was a chance for James to get out of his shell and begin to discuss what he really felt about the war. He was no longer describing the mundane events of his military life like drilling or dinner but instead he was analyzing his thoughts. James began to reflect on his situation and the person he had become.

The openness of the October 15 entry allowed James to discuss the aspect of patriotism and duty to answering the call when needed. Patriotism takes on different forms for different people. Patriotism is also unique to each time period. To James, patriotism is woven together with one of his personal characteristics of "doing what needs to be done." Earlier in this thesis, it was discussed that James believed in doing what needs to be done even if you do not want to do it or whether it is in the face of great hardship. James answered the call of the United States Army, loaded a train and headed straight to the Western Front, even if he had some reservations on whether he should be in the war or not. James, like many men that fought in the Great War, did what was needed to be done at the time. In the diary, James discusses patriotism in the form of passing it down to his children. He remarks that "my children shall be taught Patriotisms as a sort of religion as long as the stars and stripes continue to wave in the just and righteous cause it now stands for. The Army to a man stands back of it and President Wilson."[73] James had gone through a tremendous amount of hell and hardship within the last three weeks. It is the feeling of going through hell with his fellow soldiers that makes him feel a special sense of patriotism when fighting for the United States Army.

Patriotism was an attribute that he brought back to the United States. James had followed through with his promise and patriotism had become a collective memory for the Bowman family. A collective memory is "the joint memories held by a community about the past."[74] Hunt described that the First World War was remembered so deeply by soldiers and families at home that it had

---

[73] James A. Bowman. *Diary, 1918-1919*. Transcribed by Cheryl Foy and Alexander Foy.

[74] Hunt, Memory, War and Trauma., 97.

become a central part of soldiers' narratives.[75] This belief in patriotism, like memories, was passed down to the next generation. It is with my grandfather and my mother that they still carry on this belief in patriotism and one's duty to help the United States.

World War I also gave Americans a newfound sense of patriotism in trying to "defend democracy abroad." One of the U.S. Senate's most influential Republicans in determining the country's foreign policy during the war described America's involvement as a way "to preserve and make safe our own blessed Republic, to give honor and dignity and security to this democracy of ours, and to keep it is we could as our fathers transmitted it, whole and triumphant."[76] To the majority of Americans, the war was seen as a cause of defending democracy and helping our allies. World War I was the first war in 20th century American history that relied heavily on the use of propaganda to drum up support. World War I was known as "the war of the poster." Governments had commissioned artists to create posters that proposed patriotic sacrifices for good

---

[75] Hunt, Memory, War and Trauma., 104.

[76] Ross F. Collins, 2008. *World War I: Primary Documents on Events from 1914 to 1919.* Westport, Conn.: Greenwood Press., 226

citizens to support their government.[77] Some popular examples of these propaganda posters were messages on buying Liberty Bonds, the sinking of Lusitania, and the now famous, Uncle Sam's "I Want You." These posters helped channel a sense of patriotism at home for the war that pushed our need to help "defend" democracy abroad.

Patriotism in the United States also led to anger and disgust for the Germans. An editorial in the *North American Review* in February 1918 wrote,

> Our duty is to kill Germans . . . We must think in terms of German dead, killed by rifles in American hands, by bombs thrown by American youths, by shells fired by American gunners. The more Germans we kill, the fewer American graves there will be in France; the more Germans we kill, the less danger to our wives and daughters; the more Germans we kill, the sooner we shall welcome home our gallant lads.[78]

The editorial shows how propaganda painted the picture of demonizing the enemy during war. It is a reflection to how war changes the mindset of those gearing up to fight. The propaganda helps define the mentality of "us vs. them" which creates an enemy that needs to be killed because the country is no longer safe. The *North American Review* editorial article shows far the extreme side

---

[77] Collins, World War I: Primary Documents on Events from 1914 to 1919., 226.

[78] Collins, World War I: Primary Documents on Events from 1914 to 1919., 242.

of the war propaganda will reach in order to strike anger in the hearts of Americans.

As James switches topics within the entry, he begins to realize the impact that the war has had on his life moving forward.

> *I can't help but dream of the good I have derived so far out of this conflict. It has opened my eyes to possibilities of a richer life and a faith that shall linger on thru the years and with the Love of a woman so noble and pure such as I guess I know I shall be fully repaid for all these hardships and privations I've been thru.*[79]

James had been away from Evelyn for over four months and his only communication was mail that would take weeks to receive and respond. As the war began to unwind, James wrote about seeing a bright future in the wet, muddy, and desolate world that he currently inhabited. James might have felt a sense of guilt when reflecting upon his life. When he was faced with death for over two weeks, it seemed as if life would never return to its normalcy. James's tone changes in the October 15th entry compared to the beginning of the diary. In the beginning of the diary, he expressed some hopeful optimism, unaware of the consequences of war. As he reflected on his time in the Meuse Argonne, he gained perspective

---

[79] James A. Bowman. *Diary, 1918-1919*. Transcribed by Cheryl Foy and Alexander Foy.

over his life. No longer will the long days on the oil fields in Fellows, California drag on, no longer will the small fights in his marriage take old. He used Evelyn as a beacon of hope. Evelyn served as a hope for a better life than what he had been living. It would be a cliché to call the events of the Meuse Argonne lifechanging, but it had given James new perspective on a "richer life" and "the Love of a woman so noble and pure." Evelyn was the source of hope that his life could return to normalcy. In the horrors of war, it had taught James a lesson about the riches in his life that he had neglected for so long.

Through all the guilt and disgust of war, James held the Meuse Argonne in a special place within his memory. James held a certain personal pride that he was able to help the A. E. F. and the French Army push back the Germans and ultimately put an end to the war. Wilson and Tooze reflected on the ending of the Meuse Argonne Offensive in a similar fashion. They remarked that "it is no small satisfaction to know that the 364th Infantry was in it at the beginning and, during eight days of advancing and holding, contributed its share to the successful prosecution of that campaign;

to know that during the whole time we were in the line our faces were always and determinedly towards Germany."[80]

Even in having a sense of pride for helping the Infantry put an end to the war, he quickly changes tone and ends his reflection. "However, it is done and must be forgotten."[81] And with that line, James tells himself how he is going to move forward with this conflict. James moved forward with his life with going forward each day, trying to forget what happened on the battlefield of the Meuse Argonne Offensive. James did not disclose his military stories with my grandfather. He did not talk much about what happened on the Front and the only story is a vague recollection of storming a machine gun nest with some fellow soldiers. This is the last recollection of the war that James will write about aside from the letters he will send my great-grandmother. James would end quickly one of the only discussions about his experiences during the war and would take the memories of the Meuse Argonne to his grave.

As James ended the entry, he discussed to the main motivation for staying alive, his wife, Evelyn. Throughout the diary,

---

[80] Wilson and Tooze. With the 364th Infantry in America, France and Belgium, 89.

[81] James A. Bowman. *Diary, 1918-1919.* Transcribed by Cheryl Foy and Alexander Foy.

James briefly discusses the love he has for Evelyn in short and concise sentences. James writes more in the letters that are sent home which will be discussed in chapter two. James wrote about his appreciation to Evelyn, "It is to you Evelyn that I owe all these riches you showed me the open door and helped me in. I owe a debt to you I can never fully repay but by jinks. I'll keep at it and if love will ever pay the bill, I can pay quite a heap of it in time." For the next fifty years, James would go on to repay his debt to his dearest sweetheart, Evelyn.

*Oct 20-18*
*Was out of ink for a while but now I'm the proud owner of a better of native ink. I left the ward today and am now in the convalescent ward. Felt fine for a day or so then my little stomach and bowels went slightly wrong again, but they are on the road to recovery once more. My appetite vanished too and that is something rare for me. Nothing to do now but wait for peace and then home and the greatest prize of all "Evelyn"*

*Oct 24-18*
*Still in the convalescent ward and don't feel much informed had sort of relapse. The weather is so discouraging cold, foggy and wet it seems impossible to get well. There is a nice little town near here "Alenya" one can buy grapes, cakes, and candies and other eatables and have just about spend all my merger wad. Got some native candy today that was fairly good but hold the fines. The Red Cross sells Italian chocolates sometimes that come nearer to equaling our own than any I've been able to find yet. They feed mighty poor here for a man with stomach and Bowel trouble. I still can time to be homesick. I ought to write a letter but feel to blue to write. A very cheerful one. However will attempt it this P.M.*

*Oct 28-18*
*Nice day, sunshine all day and fell quite a lot better just discovered this evening that I have a few bites, I guess they came from these old blankets sleep on.*

*Oct 30-18*
*Another nice day it has been so warm tho am afraid it will rain before another day ends. I feel good but am weak yet. Think it is lack of nourishment. Our food is terribly poor and scant more like prison rations than anything else. Am dead broke too and can't buy anything. If only we could get enough to eat our morale would be a hundred percent better. I am sure a homesick boy. They called for musicians yesterday and I gave my name. I may get to stay here. I really believe I would rather get undermine such an outfit here than to return to the outfit and get all that hard work and exposure because I know I won't stand it long and then I would have to go to a hospital again. If I have to return will try and get in our own band again. I don't think I can carry a pack again on account of my shoulder. I feel that if we could get enough to eat everything would be O.K. I lay awake nights thinking of things to eat and home. I will eat when I get home. Evelyn dearest girl you will have to have a bankroll saved up to feed me on when I get home. Love will be free but eats will cost money.*

As October ended, the Great War began winding down in a similar fashion, with the German retreat and diminishing resources in terms of firepower and manpower. October also welcomed a solemn end to one of the bloodiest chapters in American military history. In the months of September and October 1918, more American soldiers were killed or wounded during these two fateful months, more "than in any month of battle during either the Civil War or World War II, making this the costly period in American military history."[82] It was during these two months of World War I that nearly 27,000 men died of combat-related wounds.[83] James and the rest of the 91st Division, including the 364th Infantry, was pulled back from the front of Meuse Argonne by November 2, 1918 ending their involvement in the deadliest American battle in United States military history. The Meuse Argonne Offensive had more causalities in the one offensive than the Gettysburg, D-Day, and Iwo Jima combined. The second deadliest campaign in United States history was the Battle of the Bulge with over 19,000 men killed, nearly 8,000 less than in the Meuse Argonne.

For a battle that swallowed up more American lives in one offensive than any other, Meuse Argonne is somewhat lost in history. In terms of military casualties, Lexington and Concord, Battle of Bunker Hill, Battle of Gettysburg, D-Day, Iwo Jima, even the Alamo which wasn't a large military campaign, is remembered in American popular culture more than the Meuse Argonne. Even

---

[82] Jennifer Keene, *American Soldiers' Lives: World War I.* Westport, CT: Greenwood Press, 2006, 20.

[83] Leonard P. Ayres, *The War With Germany: A Statistical Summary* (Washington, D.C.: Government Printing Office, 1919), 120.

World War I is forgotten to its younger brother that happened twenty-two years later.

*Nov 2-18*
*Saturday P.M. and still in camp. Haven't heard any more from the Band for position so far and no word about evacuation. Feel pretty good now. We have a stove in barracks now and it is warmer and more like a decent place to stay.*

*Nov 6-18*
*Sill here and don't know when I will get out. Food is much better and that is a whole lot of help. Weather warmer and not much rain either, some sunshine. Peace is coming closer every day. Germany is standing alone now.*

*Fri Nov 8 -18*
*Still here, that would be evacuated today but no. News has come that an Armistice has been signed with Germany, but we don't know the truth. Anyway it is just the matter of a few more hours and hostiles will cease and then Home.*

*Sunday Nov 10-18*
*Left convalescent camp yesterday afternoon, arrived at this rest camp about 10 P.M. Last night want to get out of here as quickly as possible. They don't keep anyone here long. Hope not anyway rail to get to the outfit. Germany hasn't signed yet but she will soon. I'm sure.*

*Nov 12*
*Left the rest camp on thru afternoon of the 10th and went by way of Bois-La-See near Paris to Dunkirk. We stay here in Barracks two nights and I guess we move on to the Division tomorrow. Hostilities ceased yesterday and the French were happy and celebrating everywhere last night of course we are as happy as can be too. We will soon get home now. The 91st Div is somewhere in Belgium.*

It had ended a war that saw 40 million people killed and 32 countries wrapped up into its chaos. The cumulative effects of attrition in the trenches, superior technology, and the tactical change from the Allied forces wore down the German army and its allies.[84] So when the Germans had signed the armistice, legend wrote itself into the history books as the guns fell silent at the 11th hour of the 11th day of the 11th month. James had been pulled away from the frontlines for nearly a month resting from his bout with dysentery. James remarks about seeing the French celebrate the long drawn out war. Since they arrived in Europe in mid-July, James was entering his fourth month near the Western Front. For the French soldiers and citizens, this was their fourth year fighting a war that plagued and engulfed their country. With the armistice signed, the war would soon conclude and lead to the mobilization of soldiers back to the United States would commence. The only question for James Bowman was when.

*Nov 24th Sunday*
*Have been neglecting my diary. Have been so busy. Joined the company at Mater Belgium about the 16th and have been kept pretty busy ever since marching, drilling etc. We are on the march west ward now and we think we are on the final leg of journey home. Belgium is a much nicer and richer looking country that France and the people are nicer but they haven't much eats to sell. Some towns are not damage at all but all the railroads are destroyed. The Germans are going to have some expense to rebuilt there if again.*

[84] Tim Travers, *World War I: A History*, ed. Hew Strachan (Oxford: Oxford University Press, 1998), 288.

*Rumors are afloat of all kinds but I have high hopes of getting home by X-mas.*

On November 29, 1918, two months following the Meuse Argonne Offensive, James received word from the Commanding Officer of Company F in the 364$^{th}$ Infantry. James was being recommended for citation.

The recommended citation read:

1. Although privates in the MEUSE-ARGONNE battle, September 26 to October 4, 1918, these soldiers showed unusual aggressiveness throughout the entire battle, and marked bravery and leadership in assuming command of groups.
2. In the attack of EPINONVILLE, September 27, 1918, by their aggressiveness and willingness to close with the enemy, and their indifference to machine gun fire, they set example of high conduct for which they were subsequently promoted.[85]

James was cited by the United States Army for exceptional bravery and meritorious conduct under fire. It was a matter of life and death and my great-grandfather had to act in order to save his life and the lives of his fellow soldier. When I read over the passage of his citation for bravery, I swell up with pride for my great-

---

[85] Citation from 91$^{st}$ Division. United States Army. (Private collection of Alexander Foy, 2020).

grandfather. Knowing his personality and what he wrote in the diary, James did what he had to do in order to survive. When I asked my grandpa about his father's merit in combat, James Bowman did not dive into too much detail regarding this act of selflessness to advance and protect his fellow soldiers. This was another unknown fact that my great-grandfather never shared about these actions on the battlefield could have labeled him as a hero. My great-grandfather was not one for the limelight and the recognition that few soldiers received during this battle was not something he would openly share or would he be willing to divulge any details. Like his son, James most likely would say the usual Bowman line in any occasion, "you did what you had to do and that was it." The citation is another aspect of the diary that is not discussed and gives context to how James moved on from the war and into civilian life.

*Dec-1 Meulekeke Belgium*
*We are billeted here, have been here about a week but expect to move on anytime now. This is the largest town we was every billeted in.*

*Dec 4th-18 Egem Belgium*
*We left Meulekeke eight oclock A.M. Billeted in this little bung for the two nights. I guess we are going home sometime.*

*Dec 6-18 Holsbeek Bel.*

*Arrived here about 12 & 11 today. Expect to continue the march tomorrow. About on the edge of no man's land near Ramblers. This town has been badly shot up.*

*Dec 10th- 18 Herzeele France*
*We marched across no man's land in three days, making 35-30 and 24 kilometers a day. We arrived here Sunday night. Dec 8 and everybody was all in. We rested yesterday drilled some today. Expect to move on somewhere any day. We crossed into France Sunday p.m. about 1:30. No mans land is a lonesome sight as bad as the desert.*

*Dec 11-18*
*Same place. We had a bath today and was paid tonight. I drew 246.30 francs.*

*Dec 24-18 Herzeele Fra.*
*Been in this hole all this time and we are all sick and tired of it. This morning about 4:30 the barn caught fire from our kitchen and burned burnt and the French are wild. Rec'd my Xmas package yesterday and everything was in fine shape. We signed payroll yesterday. Lots of the boys are wined up of a bit tonight Am on guard tomorrow. Color Guard Bn Hqet. It snowed this eve.*

*Jan 2-19*
*Aveze France.*
*Left Herzeele 3 P.M. Dec 30th arrived here 1 P.M. Jan 1st. rode in boxcars and went over some more of French territory. I didn't get the names of many towns we past thru. We hit the outskirts of Amiens. We hit several large places at night and couldn't get the names. Will soon be home.*

Beginning in late December, the "regiment was furnished a guard detail to patrol the Franco-Belgian border."[86] The 364th Infantry detrained at La Ferté-Bernard and began to scatter across

---

[86] Wilson and Tooze. With the 364th Infantry in America, France and Belgium, 146.

the countryside. La Ferté-Bernard is nearly in the 103 miles west of Paris, France and 263 miles west of Meuse Argonne. Companies E and F occupied one village known as Aveze, France which James identifies in the header of the entry for January 2. The two companies would later move on to St. Germain-de-la-Coudre in the first part of February.[87]

*Jan 13-19*
*Today was pay day. We have been drilling and hiking most of the time here. It rains a great deal but mostly at night. We expect to leave here in a few days.*

*Jan 28-19*
*Aveze France*
*The Division was reviewed by Pershing near Ige, yesterday. We had to get up at 4 A.M. March 9 kilometers and rode in trucks the balance. It was a cold day snowed and we had to stand in one spot for nearly 4 hrs and stood at attention so long that several men fainted and keeled over. It was after 9 P.M. when we got home. The trucks brought us all the way back. The fellows were good and sore. We had nothing to eat all day.*

The inspection by the Commander-in-Chief of the A.E.F., General John Pershing, was an extensive affair for the 91st Division. Pershing had greeted the soldiers and issued citations for the men that displaced valor in the Meuse Argonne Offensive. Sergeant Lloyd Siebert of Company F of the 364th Infantry, received the

---

[87] Wilson and Tooze. With the 364th Infantry in America, France and Belgium, 147.

Congressional Medal of Honor for his actions in the Meuse Argonne. Sergeant Siebert was in the same company as my great-grandfather and James could have possibly fought side by side with one of the most decorated soldiers in World War I history.

The cold weather had developed by the end of January and for nearly two months, James does not write in the diary during the de-escalation of war. A variety of factors could have been involved with the absence in writing since not much was going on and the cold weather could have put a damper on the motivation to write about the normal daily life of a soldier waiting to go home. It could have been the fatigue of war and the emphasis on his internal countdown clock to heading home. The diary does not give much information for February and parts of March. Although James did not write about the month of February, he would reveal his true feelings in the letters written home to Evelyn. Then word came, which held some of the greatest news that James had heard in over a year: he was heading home.

*March 14th 19*
*St Germaine France*
*We've been in this town since the first part of Feb. Have neglected my diary and all friends have felt so disgusted. Will we are all ready to leave for home, expect to go next Tues.*

With the journey coming to an end on the Western Front, Corporal James Bowman finally went home. It would be the final time that James is a soldier in the United States Army and one of the final accounts he will ever write or tell about his time overseas. In one month, James would be home in Camp Mills, where he was given the order from Colonel Lucius Bennett, to parade in Los Angeles California, and to demobilize at Camp Kearney.[88] It would be the official end of James's life in the United States Army. The official end to the Great War would not come for another three months with the signing of the Treaty of Versailles. James sent word to Evelyn that he is returning home. When he arrived back in early April 1919, the Bowman family picked up the pieces right where they left off.

[88] Wilson and Tooze. With the 364th Infantry in America, France and Belgium, 160.

# *CHAPTER 3*

## DEAREST SWEETHEART

One afternoon, I ventured over to my grandparents' house to visit and eat lunch. It was a Saturday and my grandmother had been conducting her yearly spring cleaning. When I walked into the patio room of my grandparents' house, she had two boxes on the table and told me she found some things that I needed to see. One box contained photo frames from James and Evelyn, while the second box contained a variety of items from their lives. In one plastic bag, stacked neat and tall were the letters of Private James Bowman to Evelyn Bowman. It was not just one letter but instead it was forty-three letters, folded and in their original envelopes that James had sent nearly one hundred years ago. I knew that these letters would offer a whole new perspective on James than the one developed while reading in the diary. The diary had offered one piece of the puzzle into James Bowman's experience on the frontlines and the letters would develop a whole new perspective on my great-grandfather.

In the diary, James is calculated and somewhat short with his responses. In the letters, he is completely different in the openness and great lengths that James writes to update Evelyn on nearly every aspect of his life on the Western Front. The letters will serve as a guide as James navigates the war and his marriage. The surviving forty-three letters written by James Bowman to Evelyn have a deep and enlightening meaning on his experience on the Western Front. In this chapter, I have condensed the letters to show how James would communicate with Evelyn. The letters contain a unique perspective on how James would discuss the daily life of a soldier on the Western Front and the emotions wrapped up in being away from home. In contrasting the letters to the diary, the letters do not hold back when it comes to his deep emotional connection with Evelyn.

A revealing characteristic of the James Bowman letters is the filling of space on the paper and not leaving any open gaps. In the forty-three letters, James has an ability to fill up the page from corner to corner with writing. Unlike the diary, the letters to Evelyn were detailed with the inner thoughts, emotions, hopes, dreams, and fears of the thirty-year-old private in the United States Army. From the oral interviews with my grandfather and understanding the complexity of James Bowman's shyness, it is an interesting contrast between the diary and the letters as a form of communication.

The diary was used as a piece of record keeping. In diary, James spoke in a communal voice of "we" went here, or "we" did this. The letters have a different tone. The writing is much more personal and connected. Unlike the diary, the letters were able to connect James with Evelyn and his home. For the men fighting thousands of miles away, the letters from home were a valuable piece of connection. It was the letters from home that valued highly because they contained the reassurance that they were not forgotten by those back home. These letters were a reminder of the familiar home life that they had left behind.[89]

These forty-three letters open a personal side to James that his surviving relatives never saw before. In the letters, James was a talker, and filled up the space with deep inner thoughts and feelings that he only expressed to Evelyn. The letters are written with a heavy toll on his heart, not only because of the duty that lay ahead of him

[89] Jessica Meyer. *Men of War: Masculinity and the First World War in Britain*. Genders and Sexualities in History. Basingstoke [England]; New York: Palgrave Macmillan, 2009, 15.

in the United States Army, but how he longed to get home and spend every moment with his wife. The letters help open a different side of James, one that he was not willing to show with his own diary. In the letters, he was honest and sincere. He was able to open his emotions because they were ways, he could relate to the life he left behind. The letters allowed him to connect to Evelyn unlike the isolation of a diary.

On the Western Front, the supply of paper was sparse which made James utilize the entire page. James would purchase pieces of paper from the YMCA.[90] If he were unable to buy paper from the YMCA, he would trade various items with his bunkie for some extra paper. Throughout the letters, James is requesting that Evelyn send back paper with her next letters so that way he would not run out of the precious paper. Paper was a scarce commodity for those on the Front and every piece was going to be used to the fullest. Even if James wanted the letters to remain private between Evelyn, they were eventually screened by military censors. The thought of the outside eyes of a military censor was looming large over James as he debated how much feeling and emotion he wanted to put in the

---

[90] Most letters written have a YMCA letterhead.

letter. These censors were a concerned for him as he wanted to discuss intimate details of his experience without the prying eyes of a military censor.

*Figure 4.* James and Evelyn Bowman at Camp Lewis, Washington, 1918.

A prominent theme that is presented vividly throughout the letters is James's homesick feeling of being separated from Evelyn. James and Evelyn Bowman were married in August 1917, and James had entered the United States Army a month later in late September or early October.[91] She had visited him at Camp Lewis numerous times but the expedited training and the need to get the men to the Front cut down his time in the United States. In June 1918, James left Camp Lewis to head straight to the Western Front and did not arrive back into the United States until April 1919. For nearly ten months, James and Evelyn were living apart. In the letters written home, James writes about being homesick and the longing for being reunited with Evelyn. Even though he had his comrades in the United States Army, James is alone on the Western Front and wants to desperately to get back home.

James Bowman also had a desire and need for the war to end. The perception that James gives when he writes is that he believes that the fighting is going to be easy. In the letters leading up to the Meuse Argonne Offensive, James writes in an unaware manner on where they were going to go to battle and the war will end. I believe he understood the hardships of war but the way he writes makes it seems as if he has no idea what the real cost of battle will have on

---

[91] According to a letter dated, September 19, 1918, James Bowman's one-year anniversary in the United States Army was two weeks from the date. The approximate date is the week of October 3.

his emotions. This unaware tone allows James to write in a cautious optimism. He has read about the war for the last four years, but it never seemed real. The war was a distant dream. Even as he grew closer to the Front, war still seemed like a place only found in his imagination. In the letters leading up directly before the Meuse Argonne Offensive, James writes as if the upcoming battle is a simple job: where the men will get in, do their job and then get out alive.

When reading these letters, it is important to note that we are still limited in our interpretations of what James is saying. As Alice Hickey points out in her research regarding World War II letters, "we are not as sensitive to tone changes, emotional layers and reading between the lines."[92] As I have edited the letters to exemplify James Bowman's war experience, I have realized that I am limited in how I can recreate his story. As simple as it may seem, I was not present when the letters were written, nor were these letters directed to me. The only way I can examine and analyze the letters is through my family connection through my mother and my grandfather.

---

[92] Hickey, Alice, "The Need for War Letters?" (2008). *Undergraduate Humanities Forum 2007-2008*: Origins. 6. http://repository.upenn.edu/uhf_2008/6.

Another perspective when interpreting the letters is to analyze how they "were always conditioned by the tension between being at the front and writing to those who had no direct experience of it."[93] The letters offer a glimpse to how James navigated the changing landscape of the war. As they grew closer and closer to the Front, James writes in a tone of an easy tension. He recognizes the fact that they will fight but does not fully understand what it will truly be like on the battlefield. Even though we are still limited in our analysis, the letters are rich with content on what life was like on the Western Front and on the trauma of battle and allow the reader to explore the deep human emotion of experiencing war.

In this chapter, I have selected the letters that I believe best reveal the experience of James Bowman as he navigated his way on the Western Front. The letters reveal a deeply personal side that James only showed to Evelyn. After returning from the war, these emotions were kept locked up and rarely shown to his immediate family. The letters had to be edited due to length and I have included as much detail as possible to give context to the letters. Much of this chapter will be James discussing his experience on the Western

---

[93] Meyer, *Men of War*, 15.

Front, giving him his moment to tell us how he felt through his communications with Evelyn.

## Somewhere in France

In the oldest remaining letter from the war, James Bowman begins his correspondence with Evelyn, as the 91st Division makes its way to the trenches. It has been two weeks since James Bowman embarked on the *R.M.S. Olympic* on July 12th, 1918. James writes to Evelyn in one of the first opportunities since adjusting to his new life within the United States Army. In the letter, James titles the letter "Somewhere in France" and begins to tell of his daily activities as he begins the long journey to the frontlines of the Western Front. In the July 25th letter, James has just completed the three-night and two-day caravans by rail and foot to inch closer to the Argonne Forest.

*Somewhere in France*
*July 25-18*
*No. 2*

*Dearest*

*Well I havn't much life in me today, we've just finished a long journey by rail and foot. Three nights and two days of it on half rations and no means of sleeping or resting except by falling across someone else and fight for a place to rest. Well we are billeted in a French village, in houses some of which are pretty occupied by families. It is a comical sight, I wish you could look in on the berg. But everyone is making the best of it, and I feel more like a real soldier than ever. We had a long, long march from the railroad last night after being tired out on the box car ride. I made the last half of the march on guts alone. I didn't know whether my feet were working or not. We carried full packs, overcoats, blouses and rifles. Dear I think more of my socks than ever now. So many of the fellows have blistered feet today while all that ails my feet is lack of water. Will get a sort of a bath this evening if we get our barrack bags in time. I have no clean under clothes in my pack anymore and had no chance to wash any until now. The drinking water is pretty good here. Most all the boys are drinking wine but none for me. I didn't want any of the stuff unless it is a case of absolute necessity. Soldiers are allowed to buy it here as long as they keep sober, but I can live on water, it leaves no bad effects. Have had all sorts of temptations to use it, also tobacco but I have no desire to use it whatever. They say we have to put in long hours here but I guess we can stand anything now.*

*Take the civilian and houses out of this place and it is a very beautiful country but the houses and most of the people makes it seem like stepping back 500 years. Believe me dear there is only one country and only one flag. And where I am at it. There is only one "woman". You dont realize what good eats you were getting there at Tacoma. The people are on rations here of course they are not starving but then you know what rations means. We are eating from our own commissary now and we will get enough from now on. I didn't date the other letter I wrote as I understand we wasn't allowed to but I hear that we can. This is letter number two, I forgot to number the other one too. You dont need to expect many letters as I see where opportunities for writing are going to be scarce. You write to the folks when you hear from me and keep them informed. Candy is very expensive here and hard to get. I dont know when we will get any mail nor when this will go out.*
*However in spite of all of our trials and tribulations I am in the best of spirits and have more interest than ever in the works of being a soldier. Have seen two fellows already that use to be in the 23d Co. depot Brigade when I was. They both have been on the firing line for some time and both wear the gold service chevrons. They look fine. Have heard the guns booming on the front already. We dont see any papers now and have to depend on war news from mouth to mouth the last word was that the Americans were having grand success.*

*Meet two U.S. Ambulance trains carrying our wounded to the rear yesterday. The english and French are mighty glad to see Americans trooping in. It looks good to them. Have seen a lot of German prisoners and they dont look like very wise specimens.*

*Well dear I still think and think it stronger than ever that this mess will soon be over. It looks good to me and glory be the jubilee when I get home to you again. Will be a better hubby than ever. Believe me, the Average American doesn't realize how well off they are. Especially women, over here they work harder than half the men do in America. The men that are here now, tho real men I mean will make finer citizens than ever when they get to the old home again. And I know of one person, I wont mention any name but she will get some terrible beatings. I am very tired today and half asleep will try and write more details later.*

*Have to do Military Police duty tonight. Will write soon, Give Mother a kiss and a big hug. All my love to you and God be with you.*

*Your boy Jim Pvt James A Bowman*
*Co. F. 364th Inf A.E.F.*[94]

The letter paints a picture on how James's journey will begin to develop his mind and body that of a United States soldier. The three-night journey from the rail line to the Front begins to harden the exterior body as well as strengthen the mind of James Bowman. The march tested his physical strength in order to prepare for the challenges of war. The march made James "feel more like a real soldier than ever." These strenuous activities on the Western Front

---

[94] James A. Bowman, "Letters to Evelyn Bowman" (private possession of Alexander Foy, 2020). All letters are transcribed as written with all grammatical and spelling mistakes.

began to sink in for James as he became a soldier with each day of hard and tireless work. For the men that fought in the Great War, "it was an arena in which the masculinity of those who had participated in it was defined, an experience that set them apart as a generation."[95] The war had toughen them up and given them a new sense of what it was to be a soldier and a man. In the next two months, James would be introduced to the hardships and the mundane life of a soldier waiting and preparing for war.

Marching to the Front was a shared common experience for the men of the A.E.F. The transportation system in World War I was a failure in terms of readiness to transport troops and supplies to the Front. One Corporal of Company D remarked "that he had always heard that army life would make a man of him but he was sure, now, that it would make a mule of him."[96] In preparation for the Meuse Argonne Offensive, the American troops "funneled approximately 600,000 men, 4,000 artillery guns, and 90,000 horses into the region, moving mostly at night to avoid alerting the Germans that a buildup

---

[95] Jessica Meyer, *Men of War*, 1.

[96] Wilson and Tooze. With the 364th Infantry in America, France and Belgium, 37.

was underway."[97] James Bowman was one of these men, traveling numerous miles in the shadow of darkness to the frontlines of the Meuse Argonne Offensive. As Wilson and Tooze remark, "there was nothing resembling cheering when we found we were to leave a good town and march six miles in the darkness and rain to find beds in a dripping forest."[98] The rain and constant movement made the travel component of James's war experience dreadful because the men had to shed extra gear and end up in a location with wet beds or an insufficient camp. In the diary, James describes a similar experience where he marched a strenuous number of miles just to get to a location where he fell into a deep sleep during a downpour of rain.

In the letter, James described seeing the British and French soldiers and citizens joy for the American reinforcements. France had been looked in a deadlock for nearly four years before American reinforcement. James is a soldier that is fresh off basic training where the war was very new and innocent for James. The war had consumed France for so long and the sight of American troops

---

[97] Keene, American Soldiers' Lives: World War I., 19.

[98] Wilson and Tooze. With the 364th Infantry in America, France and Belgium, 37-38.

brought hope to the hopeless. Towards the end of the letter James describes seeing German prisoners, as “not very wise specimens.” American propaganda had painted the Germans as brutes and unintelligent to drum up support to enter the war. James could have carried this same belief and hatred for the Germans as the war began to heighten. When James described the German prisoners as “not very wise specimens,” it was showing how the war was changing his mindset to define his enemy as the “other”. Soon enough, James would be fighting face to face with these “not very wise specimens.”

James also notes the differences between American and French life. He notices how the war has devastated the country and that the “average American doesn’t realize how well off they are. Especially the women, over here they work harder than half the men do in America.” Throughout the letters, James will reference the hard work of the French women and how they have aged throughout the war. He describes the French villages as being torn apart because of the war with the Germans destroying their homes to rumble and ruin. The war has torn the country and their lives apart.

The transportation system in World War I hindered the ability for supplies to enter the American war effort as some soldiers "went into battle without gas masks or overcoats, while rifles, helmets and gun oil were in short supply."[99] The long marches forced some soldiers to shed pounds of gear like extra coats or gas masks in order to make the journey in one piece. It would deeply affect the future engagement in the Meuse Argonne Offensive, and "congestion in the rear during the Meuse Argonne campaign hampered the flow of supplies to the front."[100] The congestion of supplies halted the entire Meuse Argonne Offensive because the A.E.F. were unable to funnel necessary supplies for the troops on the frontlines. The lack of supplies on the Front continued to hamper the Allied victory. The transportation of men to the frontlines was inadequate which forced thousands of soldiers to hike over forty miles to the Front in preparation for the Meuse Argonne Offensive.

---

[99] Keene, American Soldiers' Lives: World War I., 21.

[100] Keene, American Soldiers' Lives: World War I., 20.

*Figure 5.* The famous Meuse Argonne Offensive traffic jam[101]

As James begins to adjust to life on the constant move, he begins to share the small details of his day to Evelyn. In letters from July and early August, James discusses the daily life of going from one small village to another, setting up a sleeping quarters in a loft of a cow stable, where "the smell is anything but delicious."[102] James also tells of the French villagers cooking a meal for the U.S. soldiers

---

[101] Meuse-Argonne Offensive, September 26 to November 11, 1918, Scenes of Traffic Conditions, 1936; Record Group 111: Records of the Office of the Chief Signal Officer, 1860 – 1985; Historical Films, ca. 1914 - ca. 1936; National Archives at College Park - Motion Pictures (RDSM).

[102] James A. Bowman, "Letters to Evelyn Bowman" (private possession of Alexander Foy, 2020).

while some soldiers took it upon themselves to teach the old Frenchman some "naughty" English words. With every detail of his daily life, James could not shake the feeling of homesickness. In a letter written on August 4, 1918, nearly two weeks after they landed in France, he begins, heartbroken that the mail is not coming in.

*Sunday Aug 4 1918*

*This is the first chance I've had to write anymore since the other night so you see I am kept busy. We had gun inspection this morning too and have just finished my weeks washing and it is now past 11 oclock A.M. so my Sunday is going to be short. The old lady under us has just cleaned out the cow stable and has stirred up the beautiful barnyard odor . . .*

*Oh, Dear Girl, I was some disappointed by this morning, they announced right after inspection that first mail had arrived and would be given out. My spirits went sky high right away but they soon drop for sad be the story there was none for poor me, one fellow got one letter #4 and that goes to show some were mislaid. I hope I've some coming somewhere because I'm just dying to hear from you. Am pretty homesick dear but am fighting it like the very devil. Dinner is over, I wrote a little in my diary somethings I want to get off my mind and couldn't write them here. We didn't have such a bad dinner today, slice of bread, cold slaw, roast beef, gravy and coffee . . . .I've been sort of holding this letter back waiting for one as I dont think much of having our own Officers reading our letters, it isn't right but that is Army life. I would give anything to hear from you, have been worried ever since I left Camp Lewis. After you get this write as often as you can and tell the rest of the folks that you write to -to write me and I will try my best to answer all letters.*

In the first order of mail, James was disappointed at the fact that none had arrived from Evelyn. He was waiting to hear word back on her travels from Camp Lewis in Washington to Los Angeles, California.

For two months, James was not allowed to disclose his location to Evelyn due to the military censors. The journey to the Meuse Argonne Front began in the afternoon of September 13th, which required the men of the 91st Division to trek thirty miles for two days to the staging area of Meuse Argonne, the Foret De Hesse. The grueling trek for the men of the 91st Division only intensified during the build up to the Meuse Argonne Offensive. It was a march that tested the physical and mental toughness of the men that walked a combined thirty miles in two days. The men would rid themselves of extra supplies. The physical exhaustion took its toll on James, as he slept through the pouring rain without even waking up. It was in these two marches that James was growing closer to the Front.

*Somewhere in France*
*Sept 18-18*

*Dearest Sweetheart*

*Wish you could see me now, you would know why you are not going to get a very long letter this time. We are bivouacked and camoflouged in an old orchard somewhere in France and not very far from the Boche. Night before last we had a long march 18 or 20 miles with Packs and I was all in but I didn't drop out. I finished neck and neck with the rest altho there was hundreds fell out and came straggling in all the next day, some havn't come in yet. We had another march last night about 9 or 10 miles but we lightened up our load considerably, altho we were tired out before we started. We give and make camp before daylight and then about an hour or so afterwards it rains and so these last two mornings I have wakened to find myself in a puddle of water and the first impression is that I have wet the bed but later on find it is rain. I dont know what is on the program for tonight. I salvaged my overcoat, shoes, shirts and blanket. Have only the clothes I have on now and extra socks. Have my slickers yet. Just imagine me now with one suit of underclothes and you know how many I have at home?*

*Well we had to strip down on account of the long marches, it is impossible to carry so much that night we left on the march there was overcoats, shoes etc. stacked up by the thousand and scattered all along the road. I lost my shaving brush and had to shave this morning without a brush about three spoonsful of water. This is some exciting life. Havnt had water to wash with for so long I cant remember just when my face has been washed last. Oh well washing is all a habit anyway?*

*We've passed thru a number of towns that the Germans held for a while after the beginning of the war and when they retreated they destroyed all the largest buildings and the towns some are in a pitiful condition. I would like to see every German town wiped off the map. We will soon be in Germany too the way they are going now and we will remind them of it.*

*I dont know when we get any mail as we our up to where they sneak the eats up to us in the dark. I am setting on the parapet of an old trench with my mess kit on my knee and I presume it has been the scene of a battle but it might not, there are trenches, shell holes and barbed wire entanglements. I suppose by the time you get this Peace talk will be stronger than ever, and you are all reading news about our Division now so I hear? Well we are going to give you more good news to read soon and we are glad too. Those fellows that had to register recently dont need to worry much about having to go to war, they will never be needed. Well must close and get some water to drink. It is pretty scare sometimes but we are a happy bunch in spite of hardship. Love to all.*

*Your boy Jim.*

As James and the rest of the 91st Division were making their way closer to the Front, they began their final preparations for the fight. The two-month journey from the shores of France into its deep wilderness has been nothing short of routine. With the sounds of artillery overheard in the distance, the war was no longer a dream and instead it was becoming more and more of a reality.

In the September 18 letter, James's writing begins to change in tone. In the last couple of days, he has had the grueling experience of traveling nearly thirty miles on foot with heavy packs of supplies on his back. His writing changes with how he reacts to the experience of the march. He becomes crankier as the tone changes from his traditional reserved and descriptive nature. He is inching closer and closer to the front and his writing shows the form of tension that is growing. James's tone is gaining a certain perspective in the war. He is becoming more hardened because he is about to go into the fight for his life. Even daily activities like shaving, washing your face, or getting a shower is no longer a priority in his life. He is gaining a perspective of the war and seeing that these activities are no longer important in his survival.

Another aspect of the letter is how he describes the villages that he travels through on his way to the Front. He describes the towns as being in "a pitiful condition" because the Germans had destroyed them on their retreat. His tone is beginning to harden even more as he seeks revenge for these actions when he reaches the battlefield. James remarks that "I would like to see every German town wiped off the map. We will soon be in Germany to the way they are going now, and we will remind them of it." The vengeful tone of James is different than his description of the Germans in earlier letters. The tone is a longing of revenge on behalf of these French villagers that have endured great hardship and adversity for nearly four years. This description of the Germans shows how James is channeling his frustration and aggression. James is starting to speak more like a soldier that is getting ready for battle.

*Somewhere in France*
*Sept 19-18*

*Dearest Sweetheart*

*We didn't leave this place last night we actually got a night to rest and I feel quite a bit like myself this morning. It is trying to rain and I am on by back in our little puppy tent with my mess kit on my knee as usual rather a hard position in which to write a love letter but you will excuse I'm sure. My bunkie and myself picked some dry dead grass last evening to lie on, we had our blouses and slickers to cover us, I used my wool helmet for a night cap and so we slept well as we were all tired out.*

*The big guns didn't keep us awake last night. We had quite a little excitement and I will say a free show put on for us last eve, at sunset. A Boche plane hovered over us and the allied anti air craft guns were firing on it. We expect it to drop a few warm ones on us but I guess it was only taking observation. It kept out of range of the guns. They kept shells exploding all around it. Finally a French plane came over from an expedition on the German lines and the Boche beat it fast. The Frenchman gave chase but he was nearly out of ammunition and when he finished He quite the chase. We expected the Boche to come over and bomb us during the night but were disappointed, as there was nothing happened except this morning there was an extra string bombardment started on the Germans near by and it is still going on altho it has let up considerably.*

*We had breakfast at 10 A.M. today. It is sort of a lazy life this? A lot of the boys have been in the Army just one year to day. My year will be up in about two weeks. You no doubt remember the date? The attitude and conduct of the men now is practically the same as when at Camp Lewis. The fact that we are in the danger zone! The French are sure glad to see us in this part of the country. They say France will never forget and the love they hold for America will never die. They say it will soon be finished now.*

*We havn't heard any war news for three or four days but I hope the good news will continue to come in and I'm sure it will. Well I've enough water to shave in and I have to clean my gun again so must get busy. This Army is full of work. Well we should worry we will soon be going back over the Atlantic to dear old Calif and you dear. Give love to the folks and keep cuddles of it yourself. Am still dreaming as usual. Will write again the first chance.*

*As ever our boy Jim.*

By September 19, James and the 364th Infantry arrived near the frontlines of the Meuse Argonne Offensive. James discussed the current events as the Germans and American artillery fire could be heard exchanging counterfires. In the second paragraph, James described the German and French plane chase that flew overhead the positions of the A.E.F. and French armies. James described the plane chase as a "little excitement" and "a free show." Even when James saw the enemy, he still wrote in a nonchalant tone when describing the preparation of war. James even described them as having a lazy day by eating breakfast at 10 am. James is describing the events of war as if he were to describe a movie or a play. He is treating the war like a show where he could turn it on or off. The tone of the writing shapes James's perspective on the situation that he has not fully grasped the war. In a matter of five days, he will be immersed in the depths of the trenches fighting up close against the Germans. As James will soon find out, war is not simply a show where you can turn it off whenever you like, it stays on and there may never be an end in sight.

In the final letter written before the Meuse Argonne Offensive, James updates Evelyn on the conditions and experiences of life near the front lines. In the past letters dated in September, James is bringing to life what challenges he is undergoing and how life on the Front is changing as they are inching closer and closer to combat. For two months, James has sensed the upcoming engagement but has been somewhat naïve to the fact that war is around the corner. The false news spreading that the war would soon be over, created a sense of hope for James that he would not see any fighting. But as James crept to the Front, he soon began to realize that war was inevitable by the destruction of the terrain caused by the prior fighting. James writes what could have been his final letter home under what he described as "awkward conditions:"

*France*
*Sept 22-18*

*Dearest Sweetheart*

*Will try once more to write you a few news items under these awkward conditions. Breakfast is just over, my dishes are washed and put away. I suppose you think it is early in the morning, but it isn't. It is after 11 oclock we are late risers and only eat two meals a day. We would eat a dozen or so more, but we dont have the stuff to eat.*

*This is Sunday too but I guess there will be no church tho the Chaplains are right along with us. We have always wanted to get where they cant dirt drill us, just so we could rest. Well we are here at last when the bugle doesn't even dare to blow, but still we have something to complain about. This bunch is going to do some eating when we get to where it can be had. We are camaflouged in a wood now very close to the Boche. You know by that, that there will be something doing soon. I wouldn't tell you this but by the time you get this letter, you will have read about it so it won't cause you anymore worry. This wood has been shelled and shelled some time ago and it is full of shell holes, the trees are scared up and in places cut in two.*

*It is a wreck, Barbed wire entanglements everywhere and big guns boom right close by. This is real war at last.*

*We havn't been under fire yet. The other night the Boche sent about a dozen shells over our heads to a high point in over rear about 1000 yds. I guess there was a French battery there. We could see the shells explode and could hear them whistle thru the air. It gave us our first real thrill of the fray. The Boche are constantly firing on the allied planes and often pieces of the shells fly in our vicinity but so far no one has been injured.*

*Night before last we got two gas alarms and I had to wake from my peaceful slumbers and slip on my mask but one alarm was caused accidental and the other time the gas didn't reach us. The French have some big guns here that they bother the Boche with during the night. It was rather hard sleeping at first but am used to it now. This war game is some game little did I think when I was a kid and used to play soldier that someday I was going to be in a war. Well here I am and the joy is all taken out of the play now.*

*It rains everyday now, sometimes not hard but just enough to make it miserable. This morning when I got up it was nice and clear and the old sun was shining but it is raining now. This is cold wet autumn weather and not very favorable for camping, especially when one has no bed. I am getting used to it now. We often speak of the old days back home and of how we used to complain when we thot we were undergoing hardships, but we know now just about what the word means.*

*We have your sympathies I know, but no one can realize what this is like until they have been in it. I know one thing dear, it is going to make me a better contented and happier when I get home than I ever was before. You will find me very easy to cook for, that is I wont be hard to please but you will be kept busy cooking as I am going to do nothing but eat for 40 or 50 yrs to make up for lost time. We do lots of talking about eats these days, one fellow said the other night when he got back to N.Y. city he was going in a restaurant get his plate full and cup of coffee and go out sit on the side walk and eat it?*

*We got in some mail today but it hasn't been distributed yet. I hope I get a letter from my sweetheart again. Well I was welcomed with four letters from you dear and Dots and one from Sam. Your one letter, mailed at Santa Monica is sometime overdue. I suppose you have given up the nurse idea for good by this time so there is no need of me getting after you again. But you will catch it for cutting your hair off. I had to get up for a little conference and lost my pencil in the fracas so must complete this with a pen and ink is precious here in the jungles. Am glad to hear that you have been getting my letters at last. You wont get them very regular but dear please be patient I write as much as I can, we've not been on any picnic it has been work, work, work and no relief. Someday we will make up for all this in much more pleasant circumstances than these. It is raining now and two of us are trying to write in this wee tent I am on my back holding my mess kit on my stomach.*

*I am anxious to know what that is you are making and to see your new dress. I cant see how so many people take you to be so young. Well it is rather a compliment anyway isn't it? I will be celebrating my 31st birthday in a week but it will be rather a gloomy celebration. Will have to hold it over when I get home. It will be several days before you will hear from me again as I am out of paper and envelopes and have no chance of getting any for a while and in the mean time we are going to fulfill a little engagement with the Boche almost any day, but rest assured I am going to write when I will have a bit of news to tell when it is over.*

*I cant answer Sam's nor Dot's letters now so just tell them the news. You will likely be in Fellows when you get this anyway. Sam says Chas Anderson was out to Fellows on a furlough after his operation. There is an entirely new bunch there now and it would hardly look like the same old place, but we will soon be getting acquainted again. I will sure be glad too. Well dearest will have to close as I am getting cold here and must move about. Just keep on dreaming a little while longer and we will soon be together again, and all this will be forgotten. Love to all the folks and oceans of it for yourself.*

*As ever your boy Jim*

In the middle section of the letter, James writes about Evelyn's pursuit of becoming a nurse. Evelyn must have informed James in a previous letter about giving up the idea of becoming a nurse. It is unknown if Evelyn wanted to become a nurse to help in the war effort or stay local in Fellows. The entry is a unique aspect of how they are navigating their relationship thousands of miles apart. In many married relationships, a career change or milestone decision is usually discussed at length when they are together. But the separation gives a new perspective on how they discussed such lifechanging matters nearly five thousand miles apart. James seems to be somewhat against her notion of becoming a nurse by stating "there is no need of me getting after you again." The statement shows that James has had numerous conversations with Evelyn trying to stop her from becoming a nurse. It is unsure of why James was against Evelyn in becoming a nurse, but one possibility could have been that she wanted to join the war effort. James, seeing firsthand, knew that was not the best place to be in the world for her to be now. James also references that he is upset with Evelyn cutting her hair by saying "you will catch it for cutting your hair off." This was one of the ways James was able to be playful with Evelyn through his writing. It shows another element of his writings beginning to open with his tone changes in a playful manner.

James describes the change of environment that now faces him in the Argonne forest. He describes it as "this wood has been shelled and shelled some time ago and it is full of shell holes, the trees are scared up and in places cut in two. It is a wreck, Barbed wire entanglements everywhere and big guns boom right close by. This is real war at last."[103] James remarks about the two gas alarms and the German planes that fly overhead with the possibility of dropping a shell on the soldiers. James attitude towards the war is changing. Up until this point, the war did not seem real, as if it were a scouting expedition or a backpacking trip. When the artillery fire rains down and the planes come even closer, death starts to become a reality. James is no longer stuck in the cocoon of marching to the front with the war will always be in the distance.

James's tone does not change regarding whether he thinks this is going to be the last letter he ever writes. James tries to reassure Evelyn throughout this time to be patient when waiting for his letters, but he knows that this could be the last time he ever

---

[103] James A. Bowman, "Letters to Evelyn Bowman" (private possession of Alexander Foy, 2020).

writes to her again. James keeps a cautiously optimistic view of surviving the battle. James never writes about the possibility of his death in any of the surviving letters. My great-grandfather kept a tone of optimism that he was going to enter the war and come back to Evelyn.

The letter also shows James gaining a perspective of his past. He writes in the letter "no one can realize what this is like until they have been in it. I know one thing dear, it is going to make me a better contented and happier when I get home than I ever was before."[104] James shared this perspective in the diary with a similar theme of appreciating the goodness of his life back in the United States. James is also sharing this perspective with Evelyn which is a sign of his maturity in opening to his wife on the eve of battle. This feeling shows the connection between the diary and the letters as they work together to give James the opportunity to reflect and share his war experience. It gives him an opportunity to share how he is changing.

James signs off with a request for Evelyn to keep dreaming because they will soon be reunited. This final letter, sent before the

---

[104] James A. Bowman, "Letters to Evelyn Bowman" (private possession of Alexander Foy, 2020).

Meuse Argonne, is revealing for James because it is a glimpse into a moment that will forever change him. James writes the letter with hope that a tomorrow will come and that he will have time to write more once the fighting concluded. It is a letter that contains a lack of full awareness, a certain naivete about the situation that will lay before for James and the rest of the 91st Division. As the 91st Division took its position in Foret de Hesse, they were faced with a terrain of "thick, heavily under brushed and cut by numerous ravines . . . with wild, sparsely populated and poorly provided with roads."[105] James only knew the German army to be a shadowy distance away, but in a matter of one week, he and his comrades would come face to face with the German army in one of the deadliest battles in United States history.

## The Meuse Argonne Letters

The Meuse Argonne Offensive marked one of the largest military operations in United States history. As of 2019, it is still the deadliest offensive in United States history witnessing more casualties of American men than any other war. James Bowman had begun the Meuse Argonne Offensive on September 25, 1918 with

---

[105] 91st Division Publication Committee. *The Story of the 91st Division*, 13.

the 91st Division. Over the course of the offensive, James would turn 31 years old and his one-year anniversary in the United States Army. Both milestones would be the cause of celebration, but James was wrapped up in the fight for his life. In the first letter immediately following the Meuse Argonne Offensive, James updated Evelyn on his condition and the events that transpired the last couple of days.

*Oct 5-18*

*Dearest Sweetheart*

*Well I would give a great deal to be able to be with you tonight or even get you some message that I am safe and sound after the battle, but there is no way except by letter so am doing the only best way and that is writing at the earliest possible moment. We went into Battle at day break Sept 26 and kept steadily at it till Oct 4th yesterday, our Division was relieved by the (censored) a French Division. I suppose you have all read about it in the papers, and also about the removal of Gen Folty and also Col (censored) weeks. Our Regiment was scattered at the start by the enemy's Artillery fire and we went over the top in little fragments, here and there and we never got reorganized till the next day, but never the less the first day was a splendid success an example of individual fighting everybody to himself and we ran the Boche ragged. I wish you all could have seen what I saw that day, it would make you all prouder than ever of our own Yankee boys. Afraid of nothing just advancing always and what they couldn't take they went around and of course they had to give up then. We went about ten miles that day and I never hear how many prisoners we captured but we got heaps of them.*

*After that day we had it harder as Gen. Folty had muddled things up so our Artillery couldn't get passage on the roads and we had to face a peace fire from that on from the big guns. Time will not permit me giving a longer account in this letter. I borrowed this paper and so far have not been able to get an envelope. We went over the top with just our reserve rations, I took three extra pairs of socks, no rain coat, wore blouse and sweater. At night we dug holes in the wet ground and slept from exhaustion when the high explosive shells tired their d--- to find us.*

*We were under such conditions for eight days and nights and our nerves are in a very shaky condition and I think I've a few more grey hairs. We are a tattered and torn and weary lot and havn't been able to clean up yet. I shaved today, I had an awful crop of whiskers, Our Co's causality list is small compared to others and we made a very brilliant charge on a machine gun strong point and took it and win comment from higher up. Pershing sent the Division a letter of Adoration or something, it was read to us today. Well I know now what a horrible thing war is and I never thot a human being could stand up under such hardships. It is in describable and I wish the thing was over and it surely will be. We don't know much yet about what is going on elsewhere, but hear that success*

*[Ends here]*

The letter ends mid-sentence and picks up the next day on a different topic. The letter of October 5 serves as a reflection for James Bowman as he begins to process the events of the Meuse Argonne Offensive. He starts to reflect on the emotional and physical strain of war and how a human being can stand up under such hardships. In the events that led up to the Meuse Argonne Offensive, James did not fully comprehend the magnitude of war and the terror it would bring to the individual soldiers. As James attempts to put into words, "it is in describable and I wish the thing was over and it surely will be." The letter of October 5 is meant to give a quick response to Evelyn as the news of the destruction at Meuse Argonne builds.

As two weeks roll by and James begins to receive treatment for dysentery at a base hospital, he begins to write more to update Evelyn on his status. In the next series of letters, James begins to change the tone of his writing to more of a reflection piece. This reflective nature of his writing is caused by the traumatic events of the Meuse Argonne Offensive. In the end of this letter, James begins to see Evelyn in a whole new light. Before the Meuse Argonne Offensive, James would write in a different loving tone compared to his writing later in the war. In the following letter, the tone of the writing is inspired by James's belief that it was fate that spared his life in the trenches of hell.

*Oct 15- 1918*

*Dearest Wife and Sweetheart*

*I spose you will be very much surprised to hear that, I am in the Hospital but dont be alarmed because it isn't anything serious just a general complaint now a case of dysentery etc. Contracted it while on the line and after we were relieved I couldn't get it check and when the outfit started on a three day march to billets I was too sick to keep up so had to go to the Hospital. Have had some experience too have been in three different ones already, first the field hospital, then an evacuation hospital and now after a 24 hr train ride am in another one and am to get my clothes tomorrow so will soon get back to the outfit. Am feeling fair but weak.*

*I've wanted to write you sooner but didn't have paper and even now have no envelope and dont know when I can get one but will take a chance. I dont know why I never conceived the idea of having you send extra paper and an envelope every time you write. I could have written you many times more than I have. And another thing you can send me a stick of gum every time you write an I can have a chew once in awhile. I've had I think 4 sticks of gums since I've been in France. I received quite a bunch of letters from you back there in the woods and it was like a little journey into Paradise to have the pleasure of reading them all. I got to write one miserable excuse of an answer in return. Well it was the best I could do, it was cold and I was sick and everything else, was all shot to pieces from exposure and being under such a strain for so long. It is great to get into these white sheets and war blankets and get out of the rain and off the ground. It is the first chance to rest. I've had since landing overseas and I think I deserve it, but what I hated worst of all was to lose all my socks. Everything was salvaged when I entered these friendly gates and when I emerge I will have a complete new outfit, but they can never replace those precious socks dear that you spent so many weary hours knitting for me. Well I got a mighty lot of good out of them and you can feel that your labors were not all in vain dearest girl and they are very much appreciated too. Dont think of knitting anymore dear as they issue heavy socks here now and anyway the talk of Peace is so strong that we are liable to wake up any day and find the war over. In fact we thot it was yesterday and we were all in the highest of spirts for awhile but last nights paper shattered our dreams for awhile longer. However we all feel and know the end is drawing very near and I've a hunch of my own that Peace will come almost as sudden as the whole thing started. There is a lot of old magazines here and I've been reading "for the first time over here" about Uncle Sam's preparations and doings in America and it is very evident He wants to end the war just as quick as we do.*

*I just got a slip today that will bring me a Xmas package from you. You have to have it mailed by Nov. 20 so it says but by jinks if it doesn't reach you in time make them take it anyway. The size of the package and weight you can see per instructions. Now all I want in that package is all the candy you can crowd into three pounds, good solid chocolate candy and if you dont have time to make some buy it, that kind you know that is good. You couldn't send me anything that would please me more than a good feast of candy. I'm dying for it and can never get enough for a taste more than once a month. I lay awake at night and think of the day when I can get home to you, dearest and have all I want to eat and love, just love and eat till my hearts content. I get so hungry here, I'll always remember my trip to France as one of hunger. I dont think I've had a square meal since coming here. I'm sure going to make up for all this when I get home.*

*Oh yes dear I still have your rose and pictures and the little silk flag next my heart and I still have your heart because that kiss is ever fresh on the rose and I (censored) always keep it so. They cant salvage those things you know. Dear Girl you dont know how much you mean to me, I cant help but feel that I was spared out there in the Hell of fire just for you, you seemed to give me some sort of faith all along that I was going to return to you safe and it gave me courage to go on. Oh that faith is something wonderful, too big for me to explain and I cant help but know that this experience will reap us such a harvest when it is all over that will amply compensate us for all this time and money it has cost us at present. Oh for that big happy home that will soon be ours.*

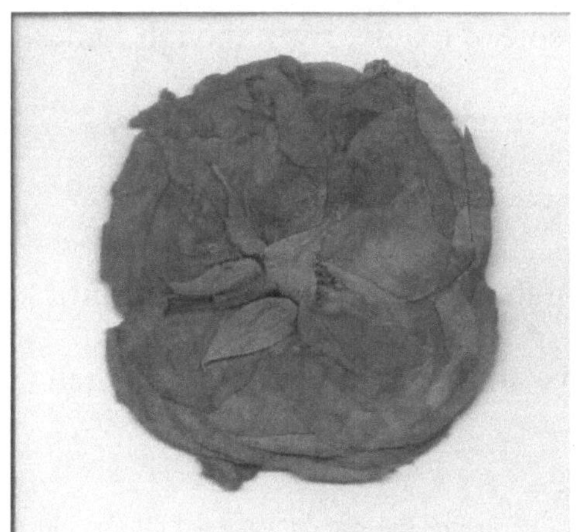

*Figure 6.* The Rose that Evelyn had sent James during World War I.

The rose that James carried next to his heart has survived nearly one hundred years later. Wrapped up in extra YMCA paper in the envelope was the rose, the one piece of Evelyn that James was able to hold when the bullets started to fly. The rose seemed like a simple gift, but it contained a much larger symbolic meaning for James as he was in the fight for his life. During war, objects are used as symbolic cloaks of invincibility as a soldier goes into battle. In World War II, soldiers of the 506th Parachute Infantry Regiment of the American 101st Airborne Division used the ace of spades symbol on the side of their helmets as a sign of good luck.[106] Soldiers have carried various objects such as a lucky $2 bill, ancestor's war medals or flags, or even stuffed animals.[107] The things that soldiers take to war carry a large significance in terms of delivering good luck and keeping them alive through some sort of magic. Even though James and Evelyn were miles apart, the rose connected them in a very desperate world. For James, that rose meant that no matter the distance or time away from Evelyn they were still together in spirit. A symbolic rose that kept him alive and "spared him from that hell

---

[106] Neil Patrick, "The connection between Ace of spades and war- it was used for good luck but also as a psychological weapon," The Vintage News. Timera Media, July 24, 2016, Accessed December 14, 2019, https://www.thevintagenews.com/2016/07/24/ace-spades-connection-war-used-good-luck-also-psychological-weapon-2/.

[107] United States Army, "Things they take to war." US Army. Published November 30, 2010. Accessed December 14, 2019, https://www.army.mil/article/48785/things_they_take_to_war.

fire." The rose also gave him a new outlook on life in the post-Meuse Argonne world. The rose was able to be a symbol of a life that still laid ahead when James returned from the Great War. A symbol of everlasting love for a woman that was waiting for his sweet homecoming.

The letters also reveal one of the most unique aspects of James's war experience. Throughout the letters, James not only seeks the love and attention of Evelyn, but the sweet and savory taste of American candy. In the diary, James rewrote a letter from Evelyn, where she discusses his need to stay away from the candy and if he indulges, he should only eat a little. When a new supply shipment enters the A.E.F. camp, James wanted to know if candy came in, along with letters from back home. In the direst of situations, James cherished the little things in life, like candy, that brought him joy and kept him deeply rooted and not losing a part of himself. Candy brought joy and solace in James's bleak Army life.

*Figure 7.* An example of candy deliveries by the American Red Cross[108]

*Oct 16-*

*Had to postpone my letter yesterday for want of paper, and now today just as we have finished dinner and wondering how we are to spend the afternoon along comes this gift from the good old Red cross and now I can write to my letter Hearts content. I wanted to write so bad yesterday, was just in the right spirit all day. Have felt so lazy and drowsy all forenoon. I will try and shake off the spell and give you my best. It is the best chance I've had to write since coming to this Land of Hunger. It may seem to you that I am always hitting France and its People. Well I dont mean it that way.*

---

[108] Photograph No. 20805710. "American Red Cross - Miscellaneous - American Red Cross furnishes chocolate. Close up of hand grasping chocolate showing label "Compliments of the American Red Cross" A.R.C. Field Hospital No. 328, 82nd Div., Varenne-en-Argonne, Meuse, France." March 1919; Records of the War Department General and Special Staffs, Record Group 165. National Archives at College Park, College Park, MD.

*Recently we have come in contact with the really better sort of French and when coming to the Hospital I saw some very pretty country, and in other words my horizon has been somewhat from deved. France and all her people deserve nothing but praise for the wonderful stand she has made in this struggle. They have suffered and bled and are still fighting like devils and will continue till victory is ours. They shall always be the warmest of friends. France and America you mentioned something about my going to Church so much over here. Well I havnt been, I've just had the opportunity of hearing our Chaplain, "Wilson" three times over here and as I like his talks so well I couldn't resist going. They are always so different than what we hear in the Churches. A preacher of any congregation is so handicapped by certain creeds and doctrines laid down that He cant preach pure religion but just a compound that has been made out for him ages past and has been preached over and over so many times that we know it all by heart. But our Chaplain talks to a crowd of many creeds or rather born of many but in reality now just one and that can easily be summed up in two or three words, and that is what we are all fighting for now. He doesn't tell us to be afraid of Hell fire & so forth, but just what I call plain every day out doors stuff.*

*So far I've only heard the band play twice so you see our entertainment over here is sufficient chiefly by the Boche. I understand the Band master was around our Camp and got my name again the day before I left but I didn't get to see him. I heard the Band suffered losses while aiding in caring for the wounded. I understood that they didn't have to do that but it seems they do. Well I dont expect to get in anyway. I was acting Corporal when I got sick and now I spose I'll even case that job when I get back. I hope not tho I need the extra three dollars that I would get if I was to get a warrant. Maybe my chance will come yet.*

*Yesterdays papers brought very encouraging news that Austria and Turkey are sort of dickering for separate peace. I feel that the end of real fighting is very near and it has started me to dreaming and building air castles on that wonderful home coming more than ever. We are going to face a period of a little uphill work and we will have to grit our teeth and toe in. We are not so very much in debt now but we will have to go deeper in order to start house keeping again but dearest love, a little lesson in thrift is going to be one of the best things that ever happened to both of us. Me especially as I know you care more for the value of money than I do. I've always tossed it right and left and let the devils do as they pleased, but I've learned my little lesson, it has been burned in and I'm not going to divine anything but profit by the experience.*

*Anyway dear we are going to be just as happy and I dont see why we should not be far happier while scrimping and saving along, knowing all the while that we shall soon be out of debt and then have a little something all our own. It is the only way to be and after we work hard and get me into our own then we can appreciate it and enjoy life just that much more. And just think dear, all that time our love will be ever with us and growing and drawing interest just like money and to live and work with each other knowing all the while that we are serving each other what more of a Paradise could we ask? We are truly grateful for Sam's help, I tell you there isn't many Brothers like Sam and we owe him more than money but our home shall always be ready to Welcome him. I hate to see Hausts leave 5c. We may not go to live there tho we cant tell yet. Well dearest of all I must close and get this Xmas slip off. Put plenty of string around the package.*

*Love to all and many mountains of love to you, as every your boy*
*Jim*
*Pvt James A Bowman Co. F. 364th Inf. A.E.F.A.P.O. #776*

*Will write as soon as possible*

The rumors began to swirl as news spread that Austria-Hungary and Turkey, two of the main instigators of the War, began to broker peace deals to escape the stalemate and costly war. As the War in the East began to wind down in fall 1918, the Austro-Hungarian empire was battling against many provinces that desired to become independent. Charles I, the Emperor of Austria-Hungary, had turned over control of the military to the failing German army. As they were no longer able to drum up public support of the war and the failing victories on the Eastern Front, the mighty empire of Austria-Hungary fell apart in the fall of 1918.[109] Two weeks after the rumors began, Austria-Hungary signed a peace deal on November 3 withdrawing from the war. The Ottoman Empire faced a similar fate as Austria-Hungary with the British soldiers pushing back Turkish positions through the south Eastern Front. On October 30, the Ottoman Empire signed a peace deal with the Allies, relinquishing control of their army and territory.[110]

In the October 16 portion of the letter, James refers to Chaplain Wilson, the newly appointed Chaplain right before the Meuse Argonne Offensive, Chaplain Wilson would go on to co-write the *With the 364th Infantry in America, France and Belgium*, which served as a key source of information for this thesis. Wilson was a man that my great-grandfather admired in the desolate days of the Meuse Argonne Offensive. James might have been searching for

---

[109] Tom Pendergast, Sara Slovey, Sara Pendergast, and Christine Slovey. 2002. *World War I*. Detroit, Mich.: U.X.L., 103.

[110] Pendergast, Slovey, Pendergast, and Slovey. 2002. *World War I*. Detroit, Mich.: U.X.L., 118.

meaning after his world was shattered after seeing so much devastation and chaos on the battlefield. Chaplain Wilson brought solidarity and unity to men experiencing the trauma of war. James describes the Chaplain's talks as being a unifying voice to men of different creeds. "Chaplain talks to a crowd of many creeds or rather born of many but in reality now just one and that can easily be summed up in two or three words, and that is what we are all fighting for now."[111] The hardships of war can bring individuals together and unite them under a common purpose. Chaplain Wilson was able to bring together men from different backgrounds and converting these deeply traumatic events into some form of meaning.

In the search for meaning, James becomes more critical of organized religion and its approach to preach fear of "Hell fire & so forth." He recognizes the fact that a preacher of a congregation is limited in their approach to connect on a spiritual level with these men that have gone through hell. The men of the 364th Infantry wanted to find some form of peace after going through the hell and fire of the Meuse Argonne Offensive. Wilson can give these men a broader sense of religious practice than they probably would have

---

[111] James A. Bowman, "Letters to Evelyn Bowman" (private possession of Alexander Foy, 2020).

never realized without the war experience. My grandfather described James as a "God-fearing man." My grandfather said that his parents never really went to church instead they were focused on the teachings of the Bible and allowed their actions to carry forward their faith. The war itself could have given James a new sense of spiritual being. It could have given him a new perspective that religion is the actions you have taken in life and the way you live. The last thing James wanted to hear was that he needs to save his soul from the depths of hell. He had accepted the events of the Meuse Argonne Offensive for what it was, war. Chaplain Wilson was able to preach a form of spirituality that allowed these men to connect to each other, to their past, and to their future no matter their religious background.

In one of the longest writings James wrote in a two-part letter, on October 18 and 19, he begins to talk about the harsh winter ahead in the countryside of southeastern France. It is the third letter that James is sending home post-Meuse Argonne that James reveals the traumatic experiences of mentally and emotionally coping with the war.

*France*
*Oct 18-18*

*Dearest Sweetheart and Wife*

*Will undertake to send a few more lines this morning but it is so cold my fingers are stiff so I know this will be another of those poor letters. I see this morning that my other letters with the Xmas slip in hasn't been mailed so my hopes of getting a Xmas package from you have about all flown away. My only hopes are now that actual fighting will soon be over and then they may lift the restrictions and allow more packages to be sent over. It seems pretty tough that you folks at home can't send us little things once in a while but when we consider the big mass of men that are here and the labor and ship room it takes that is needed for far more necessary supplies I guess it is our solemn patriotic duty to let it be that way and be contented that we have the privilege of writing as often as we can.*

*The Gov. has a big job on its hands to feed, clothe and keep this big Army in all other materials. And I want to say that it is doing it fairly well too. It is a big job. I got my new clothes and got up yesterday, felt fine except a little weak. I ate a large supper last night and I feel fine and dandy this morning, I expect will leave for the convalescent ward tomorrow and it will be a few days yet before I reach the old Company again. Was issued two suits of new woolen underwear, good stuff, slightly lighter in weight than what we had at Camp Lewis but it is better stuff. Have a new over coat everything new. I liked my stay here, it gave me a much needed rest and a little time to think. Have let me complaint and that is while I was in bed I didn't get enough to satisfy my hunger, but that was the best thing for me as I havn't much control over my appetite these times. Everything tastes good now since I am feeling better and I would eat enough to kill me if I had it. You will find me a very easy man to cook for when I get home. I eat anything now and quantities of it. So dear, all the trouble you will have is finding enough to fill me up. When we returned from the front they had all sorts of eats for us at our kitchen but I couldn't eat much so it hurts me to think of the lost opportunity to enjoy eating. Well dear we can eat & eat to our hearts content soon.*

*The war is fast nearing its end, Turkey has just about quit, when Austria and Turkey both quit then Germany has little left but to surrender, and it wouldn't surprise me a bit to see her quit any day as it is. The sooner she does the better for her and surely she sees it too. There will be many a heart made glad for Xmas should fighting cease before then, and we have many reasons to believe it will, yet we will have to stay here sometime after that, but that will be easy compared with fighting. Believe me I am dreaming a lot these days about the home going. I guess it is because I will be coming home soon.*

*Have been sending your mail to Fellows, trusting that you would be there, but in case you are not they will be sent to you. I am anxious to get back to the Co. for I know I will have a stack of letters there from you. And that will be far better than good eats. That money Sam sent me will come in handy I reckon as I've missed the pay this month so will not get paid till next month. I still have plenty and may not need it. I have to buy several small articles as I lost pretty right everything I had. I must go now and hunt a shaving brush, and whatever else they have to sell I need also. I must get my fingers warm, will tell you about it later. The Red Cross operates a small canteen here but dont know what they have to sell. It is darned hard to buy things here It isn't like the good old U.S.A. Well so long will come back a little later.*

As the chapter of Meuse Argonne begins to close, James can look past this traumatic event and his hopes for a better future with Evelyn. In the closing paragraphs of the October 19th letter, James begins to dream about a future. He dreams about starting a plan on how the couple how the couple will move forward with what little money they have left after the war. James moves from recording the mundane events of military life to discussing his future with Evelyn. It is a shift of maturity that James is growing up and read to move on from the war. The letter begins to shape his perspective on lost time and the ways he can make it up. Over the next couple of months, James discussed various financial moves that they should make in order to buy a home, and what jobs are available for Evelyn. It was a way they could start to rekindle their relationship after all the lost time. James remarked that this series of events will be the very last time anyone will be able to separate them as a couple. It was a promise that James kept for the rest of his life, and no one was able to separate them until Evelyn passed away in 1967.

*Oct 19*

*Well I didn't get back to write anymore yesterday. I managed to get a shaving brush, tooth paste, ink and a little bit of cheap native stationary. I came pretty near getting a cake of chocolate at the Red Cross, had to stand in a long line and when I finally got to buy it was finished. They sure go wild over a little chocolate here. Yesterday for dinner they gave us corned beef, and for supper salmon and it put my stomach out of whack. That is a great bill of fare for a hospital.*

*Winter is coming for good I guess, it is always raining and cold. I dread to think of it too, but if we dont have to fight and can be quartered in billets it wont be so bad, in fact it would be Paradise compared to fighting. My hopes are higher than ever now that fighting will cease soon. Last night papers sure bring encouraging news. You mentioned somethings about sending me papers. I dont know what to think about it. It is nice to have something to read. If you can send me the Literary Digest every week it will be better than a paper and I can see what the rest of the world is doing. See what you think of the situation and if it doesnt cost too much try it out. Since coming to the hospital I have read my first magazine since coming across. I dont care about stories but just the doings of the world.*

*My hands are so cold I can hardly manipulate the pen. Am such a beautiful penman too it is a shame. Guess I will go back to bed and keep warm. I had a bunch of crazy dreams last night. In fact I've done a lot of dreaming since being at the front, due I guess to the condition my stomach is in, but I dream every time I fall asleep and they are the craziest too. Last night was the first I've slept any length at a time. I went to bed before dark and slept till midnight. Believe me that little stay we (censored) sure had its (censored) me in several ways. You can have no idea as to what a (censored). I hope I dont have to go back and I dont think we will, tho we cant tell just yet. I dont know where our outfit is yet. I am not progressing very rapidly with my French. I lost the book Ares gave me. I dont take any interest in it anyway, I will have my hands full if I speak English correctly, I guess you know that?*

*Anyway I have for too many golden prospects ahead after the war is over to worry about a little old French Language that will never do me any good after I get home. It would be great to have a little California sunshine here these days. Dinner is over, we had a little helping of spaghetti and some sort of tasteless pudding, bread and black coffee. My appetite is all gone today and I didn't enjoy the repast. I feel better tho as the day progresses. I leave this ward tomorrow for the convalescent camp don't know how long we will be there but it wont be so very long. I am pretty dog-gone homesick but they dont treat much cases in this hospital. In fact there is only one place that can give relief for that and that is a little bungalow way off, many miles from here, full of warmth and cheer and love in large clear letters. Can hardly wait till the time comes. It seems like we have always been apart and always planning on our meeting again and then when the time did finally come it was only for a short time and thru we had to part once more.*

*Well me thinks dear, that this next meeting will be the last time they can separate us and we can go on, uninterrupted in our little home building. I often wonder just how comfortable a little nest we would have by this time if this war hadn't of taken it from us. I know it would have been all that Labor and Love could make of it in that time. Yet it isn't really right to call it Labor, Love is sufficient to call it because where there is love labor is nothing short of pleasure. And there is no end to the little things we can do towards improving a home and making it more comfortable day by day. It is certainly one of the grandest of the pleasures of Life and those that never had a home nor will never have one have surely been deprived of Life's most precious possession.*

*Often think of our future these days and wonder what just what sort of a course we should choose for our voyage. We started in our journey with out a compass nor chart, just drifted with the tide and now when we get our worldly possessions together again and ready to continue the journey it is our "solemn" duty "so to speak", to choose a course and a sailing point. There are opportunities of all kinds and all it takes is a little determination and some hard work, but Love is the main factor always and where ever love is no work seems too hard nor any sacrifice too great. We can always be saving a little as we go along and it is the little things we save each day that counts up big and this war is teaching most of the world, especially the United States a very costly lesson in thrift, and I am one of the benefiters too. Well the first thing is to plan for a nice comfortable home and we must have an income of some kind so when we reach that age that we want to let up a little on our labors, "not that we want to but age says we must" we can have something to keep the wolves away and we need never worry.*

*Oh I guess we will have plenty to do alright and it is all going to be one big whirl of pleasure in the doing and one thing I'm absolutely sure time will never drag on our hands and no kinds of labor will ever become a dendgery to us. Life will always be just one big day of gladness. It makes one sick to think of the good money I've wasted in my life. It has been a very dear lesson and I am ashamed to think of it now. Well I am a young man yet and there is no reason to feel discouraged, many men are failures at 45 and even 50 years and still win out later on. Have an Uncle in Colorado that was almost a pamper at 40 and today he has a very nice home and some land besides a good position. So dearest Forever we have the world to live in and no limit to what we can do and it looks to me like "golden prospects" ahead for us, even tho we start in debt we should never feel discouraged. Well I am very anxious to get home and get started, and just hug and kiss you till you squeal for mercy. Must close and get this mailed. Love to all and oceans for yourself. Will write very soon.*

*Your boy Jim*

## Coming Home

As November and December passed, the prospect of James leaving the Western Front and heading home just in time for Christmas emerges as nothing more than a dream. In nearly every letter written in the months of November and December, James holds on to hope that they will eventually be on their way home in time for the Christmas season. But as he soon realizes that the transportation system was depleted by the war, his outlook to return home changes from optimistic to knowing that it could be many months until he is headed home. As Christmas passes and he receives the gift box from Evelyn, the waiting game continued through the cold, snowy, and frigid French winter.

With the waiting game continuing, James writes in the harshest and brashest tones ever appearing in the letters as he seethes with anger at the American government, especially the military high command. As the prospect of going home early and in time for Christmas passes, James realizes that those in power are playing a political game instead of doing everything necessary to bring the troops home, two months after the Armistice. In the previous letters written in the months of December and January, James understood the logistical nightmare that laid ahead of the A.E.F. with the destroyed railways left behind by the German troops. The letter of January 26th is different in the sense that James does not relent in his dissatisfaction with the representatives in Washington as they prolong and attempt to broker a peace deal.

*Figure 8.* A letter mailed by James A. Bowman to Evelyn on January 10, 1919.

*Aveze-France*
*Jan 26, 1919*

*My Sweetheart Wife*

*Once more I take up the pen in your behalf. I was writing to Dad and Mother Bowman last night and while rummaging thru my personal* *effects I found a letter I had written to you Jan 10$^{th}$ and somehow had over looked mailing it so I put it in the mail sack today and no doubt you will get this one at the same time. I havn't rec'd any letters from you for several days except old ones that have been sent to hospital. I take it to mean that you are expecting me home any day and dont know whether to write or not. Please dont let that interfere dear girl just write on and on because I will get them anyway and there is a chance that we may go to Russia or be held here indefinitely altho I'm praying for home every day and will be broken hearted if we dont get home soon.*

*The pros for an early trip home are not so promising as a month ago and I feel pretty blue about it but what you and I think of it doesn't matter one bit with the men that are detaining us here. The situation in Russia has the most important part of this world drama and I dont expect to see any combat troops sent home until they come to some sort of an understanding with the Peace Conference. This is one devil of a mess that we got into and it is going to take some time to straighten things out. They are playing politics at home new and jumping at each others throats and throwing mud. It is a very poor time "when the nation faces such a crisis" to play the dirty game. It is the duty of all Public men that really have the interests of the nation at heart "instead of their non financial affairs" to pull steadily together in spite of party creeds. There has been much good American blood spilled and many lives sacrificed for a noble cause over here and it seems to me they are too rapidly forgetting the cost. There are over two million American citizens over here that have sacrificed much for the nation and it is the first duty of those wrangling politicians at Washington to stand together and get this business settled and get us home.*

*They are hot and heavy on Wilsons heels for coming over here. All the rest of the civilized world is glad of it. Surely there is no one else that is as fit to represent the United States as Wilson and things should run along in Washington just the same. There is no one living that is above criticism and it is right in its place, but they carry it too far. They are spending too much time handing each other bouquets at the conference but guess they have to get acquainted. If they had to live under such conditions as we do while they are doing their drinking I think they would get down to business quicker and get themselves home. They dont have any conception of what this sort of life is and there for they don't care. They are having banquet theater parties and the best kind of fun while we shiver 24 hrs a day and wonder or try to wonder when we are going home. I often wonder just how many men sitting in that conference have sacrificed anything in the war "anything compared to what us poor men that have been in the army these last seven months have"? Those men that are raising so much cain in Washington I would like to see thru them and see their motives. I'll wager they are selfish ones and not from the heart.*

*Well I am going to keep as stiff an upper lip as I can and smile and keep sweet till the times does come when we can go to our happy homes. I hate to think that the Army is making a grouch out of me but we have to do so many crazy things it drives us to exercise that one big privilege of a soldier, that is to growl, swear and cuss like a man. We were to Pass in Review before Gen. Pershing last Friday and were set to get an early breakfast but it was called off at the last minute. Now tonight word comes the big event will be pulled off tomorrow so I will have to get out at 4 a.m. in the morning. These last few days are pure and cold. It snowed some last night and today and it looks like more tonight. We had breakfast at nine this a.m. and I walked into La Ferte Bernard to the Y.M.C.A. but it was crowded and I couldn't get a place to write so by and by came home for dinner at three P.M. I was reading in the Sat eve. Post last night where we get tea or coffee, ham, jam and bread every morning for breakfast. It was written by an Officer and possibly he does but we don't. The only ham we ever got was brought out of the Company funds Xmas day and I could eat all the jam at one meal that I've ever been served with my rations. And it was a long, long time we never saw white bread as he says we had it regular.*

*Why do they try to misrepresent such things to the folks back home? If they are ashamed to tell the truth they might to keep still. That is one thing that made the Y.M.C.A. so unpopular with the boys was the way they advertised in the states what wonderful things they were doing at the front and the fact is they done nothing. While I was at the hospital I talked with fellows from almost every organization that had been to the front and they all tell the same story. We often see articles in the papers and magazines about how the A.E.Fr. are enjoying themselves in Europe and what they eat etc and then the howl sets-up. The most of those reports comes from the bomb proof jobs behind the lines. They ate the jam and go to the leave areas and do most of the writing. Wait until the combat dough boys get home and hand in their report.*

*La Ferte Bernard is a good sized little French town. They have two banks there and some fairly nice stores for a town of it size in France. They are sure loaded up with stuff to sale the American. There isn't any lace for sale here like in Belgium. I havn't brought your souvenir yet I don't know yet just what it will be. There are lots of pretty things in this town and I suppose this will be the last town we will have any privileges in as when we get to the seaport we are kept in quarantine and sterilized before we go home, so next payday Jim is going out to buy his sweetheart a little souvenir. I got some blue ink over there and it works better in my old pen, a little bottle that holds about a table spoonful I paid 12 ct for it. It ought to be good. We will soon be handling real money again, this French money is more like a joke to us than money.*

*The latest report is we get three months pay when discharged. It should be six. It would take it all to rig out in civilian clothes. The first thing I will have to have is a pair of shoes because I know I will never get my old english shoes on I left behind. I can wear out my suit tho that is one thing I wont need right away nor underclothes. If I remember right I have plenty? Well I guess it will be warm weather by the time I get home so I can go barefooted and won't need many clothes. I've been going to write to Sam for some time but as long as you see him often I will put him off till I pay off some other letters I owe.*

*In regards to those portable houses I guess you are right about the other house costing as much in the end. What discouraged me before dear was the cost of erecting after the stuff was delivered, but for a small house the kind you have planned now and I guess that what we had better start in with the cost wont be so high and will look much better when up. And there never was a house yet that couldn't have an addition put on somehow. I often, yes very often dear think of what a cozy little home we would have had by this time if it hadn't been for this old war. Those were the busiest and for the happiest days of my life and I can never be contented until we get together again and happiness takes up where it left off. Oh your little bank roll is going to suffer when I get home. You will have to tighten up on the old man or he will spend the rolls. Those Darrow boys will soon be big enough to support themselves and the Father can quit work. Is my little Dot growing like a bad weed or is she the same sweet girl I left? There will be a great change in the kids to me. They will seem like grown up when I finally get there. Well Dearest lover time is pressing so I must close the page and retire. Will write soon. Love to all and always of ocean of it for yourself . . . ..? Yes*

*The boy Jim*

The 91st Division was constantly moving from one small French village to the next which threw the entire mail delivery system into disarray. James was growing ever frustrated with the Army's lack of urgency in sending the troops home. The frustration soon grew into disgust as the tired and worn-out soldiers were ready to go home but those in Washington believed in a different timeline than those on the frontlines. As the Armistice was signed, it seemed as the war was over in the court of public opinion but for the men still overseas, the war was not over until they were home. The men of the 91st Division finally fulfilled their inspection on January 27, 1919 by the Commander in Chief, John J. Pershing, in a muddy and snow melted field.[112]

---

[112] Wilson and Tooze, With the 364th Infantry in America, France and Belgium, 152.

James refers to the possibility of being stationed in Europe or sent to Russia for a long period of time. Although James would eventually go on, many soldiers in the A.E.F. would be sent to Russia in a mission to support the anti-Bolsheviks fighters in Siberia and guard giant arms caches in Archangel and Vladivostok. It was the U.S. Army's 339th regiment that was chosen for the deployment because they were mostly from Michigan, "so military commanders figured they could handle the war zone's extreme cold."[113] These U.S. soldiers would stay in the region until January 1920 in a peacekeeping role during the Russian Civil War. Their role is a debated issue on whether it was necessary for these American soldiers to play "peacekeeper" in the chaotic times of the Russian Civil War.

In the February 16th letter, James writes about the U.S. Army's effort to mobilize in order to bring the troops home. The letter also reveals James's attitude shift toward the United States Army, political, and religious authority.

*Feb 16- 1919*

---

[113] Erick Trickey, "The Forgotten Story of the American Troops Who Got Caught Up in the Russian Civil War," Smithsonian Magazine, Smithsonian Institute, February 12, 2019, https://www.smithsonianmag.com/history/forgotten-doughboys-who-died-fighting-russian-civil-war-180971470/.

*St Germaine France*
*My Dearest Sweetheart*

*I wonder what you are thinking about me for not writing for so long? Well we moved from Aveze sometime ago, but not very far, just some 8 or 9 miles and settled down here in this place to rot awhile longer. We had to move to make room for some of the engineers. I dont know whether we will ever get home or not, sometimes I doubt it as the time drags on so heavily and we are no nearer home than when the Armistice was signed. I havn't written a letter since arriving here have been so blue and disgusted and we've no place to go to write like we had at Aveze.*

*There is a small Y.M.C.A. here but it is always crowded and air tight. I hate to stay in it long enough to write. Hope you will forgive me dear. I havn't been receiving any mail at all, I guess you all are expecting us home any day and think it useless to write. No one is getting any mail so that seems to be the case with others besides ourselves.*

*We all expected to be home by this time, but somehow we are not and we have no explanation of the matter. It doesn't seem to be of very much importance to those in authority whether we get home or not. Think what an awful debt they are piling up day by day and we will have to help pay it after we get home. If they only had to live as we do they would change their minds mighty quick. I never saw a more disgusted and homesick bunch of fellows in my whole life. See by the papers that the boys are still lodging complaints about the treatment they received over here. I guess there has been a lot pulled off over here that the home folks dont know much about, but they will hear it all as the boys gradually drift in. There is a certain so call prominent Military man that is talked of as a Presidential possibility but his chances of winning are going to be mighty slim if these doughboys are going to have any influence . . .*

*Well I heard a little of that Minsters talk, got disgusted and walked away. He is in the service of the Y.M.C.A. now. All he had to say was in defense of the Y.M.C.A. and then a lot of riff-raff about our spiritual welfare after we return to civil life. That doesn't interest me one bit. There are all sorts of preachers after us now it seems they are very much concerned about how we are going to behave when we get home. They are afraid we will be blood thirsty I guess. Well I say if they would come and give us socks, a little candy and other little luxuries things we didn't used to consider as luxuries but we do now. I think our spiritual welfare would take care of itself. Some of those religious sharks make me tired.*

*Our Regimental Chaplain is getting up a history of the 364$^{th}$ from its infancy at Camp Lewis up to embarkation on our homeward trip. I have subscribed for a copy. I hope it is good and have faith that it will be. I often wonder if you every got my letter with the list of pictures I sent you to order. Well if you didn't I have the list and can order after I get home. Would like to go over the same ground we covered in the Argonne battle once more. We've all talked the battle over so many times. But I wouldn't stay here a second overtime to get to see it. These days are dragging so slow and heavy and we are worried to death by inspections etc. I wish I could hear from you and fined out how you are feeling. They are sending troops home all the time that never saw the front I think we should go first. Well sweetheart if there is anything left of me by the time I get home I'll promise to be a very happy boy but I feel like the time will never come, forgive me for not writing often I couldn't get myself at it. Will try and write soon.*

*Always your boy Jim*

The month of February was filled with more waiting for the men of the Meuse Argonne Offensive. As the 91$^{st}$ Division made its way to the La Ferte Bernard area, "much attention was paid to washing of clothing, training the men in ceremonies, and in keeping them occupied to prevent homesickness."[114] As James points out in his letter, one of these activities to keep them occupied was the talks

---

114 91$^{st}$ Division Publication Committee. *The Story of the 91$^{st}$ Division*, 81.

of the ministers that were ever so focus on "a lot of riff-raff about our spiritual welfare after we return to civil life . . . very much concerned about how we are going to behave when we get home."[115] The growing distrust with those in power kept escalating for James as they kept making empty promises that only furthered his anger in the stalemate of his deployment home. Even when the spiritual leader of the camp was focused on taking out their bloody thirsty nature, James was focused on going home and getting some American candy.

In one letter, James opens his objection and criticism about the military, government, and organized religion. Usually refrained in his cynicism, James unleashes a scorn of distain on the powers that continue to keep him idle in France. The first target of James's disgust was the United States military and the inability to send them home after the fighting has ceased. The men of the 364th Infantry expected to be home by February, but no explanation was given on why they remained in France for three months after the Armistice. In a very short time, James had lost his innocence and trust in believing in the powers of the military. As the days continue to pass, James

---

[115] James A. Bowman, "Letters to Evelyn Bowman" (private possession of Alexander Foy, 2020).

was beginning to see the debt piling up from keeping the A.E.F. in Europe. James became bitter when he started to see how these soldiers would eventually have to pay off the debt of this war when they get back. The men that would fight in this war would eventually carry another burden when they arrived home.

The bitterness of the World War I generation did not just end when they left the Western Front. These men would return home with the promise of a cash bonus, which would be compensation for their time overseas. The Great Depression would hit in 1929 and most of these men that fought in the war would never get the money they were promised – and deserved. In 1932, a group of veterans in Portland, Oregon, led by Walter Waters, began a mission to lobby for early payment of the war bonuses.[116] These group of veterans would eventually become the Bonus Army and attracted over 20,000 veterans to Washington, D.C. After a few weeks, the Army was sent in to disperse the camp of the World War I veterans. News traveled throughout the country of tear gas being thrown at World War I veterans and General MacArthur driving out the troops "that had

---

[116] Joe Richman and Samara Freemark, "The Bonus Army: How a Protest Led To The GI Bill," National Public Radion (NPR), National Public Radio (NPR), September 11, 2011, https://www.npr.org/2011/11/11/142224795/the-bonus-army-how-a-protest-led-to-the-gi-bill.

won the first World War."[117] Four years later, WWI veterans received their bonuses, seventeen years after the war had ended. The stalemate of sending the troops home along with the delay of their bonus checks, carried a bitter feeling towards the war and the government for the millions of World War I veterans that sacrificed their lives for the war effort.

The letter also shows the change in James's spirituality throughout the war as he no longer wants to hear about how he must change when he arrives back into civilian life. The YMCA minister seemed out of touch with James and the rest of the men. The minister was more concerned whether these men that have been trained to kill for the last couple of months, would be able to become full functioning men of society. It seemed that the minister wanted to focus on their spiritual wellbeing through faith. For James, one way to transition back to society was to give the luxuries they enjoyed before the war with socks and candy being a good start. The change in James's tone showed his distrust in the minister. James had walked away from the minister because he was disgusted with the

---

[117] Joe Richman and Samara Freemark, "The Bonus Army: How a Protest Led To The GI Bill," National Public Radion (NPR), National Public Radio (NPR), September 11, 2011, https://www.npr.org/2011/11/11/142224795/the-bonus-army-how-a-protest-led-to-the-gi-bill.

messaging f saving their soul and turning them away from becoming blood thirsty animals when they returned home. This letter was the first time that James had changed his tone and message about higher authority. Life had changed for James since he arrived on the Western Front, he lost his innocence and gained a seething bitterness towards those of authority. He was tired of "religious sharks" telling him to repent in order to make sure his soul was clean when he returned home. But war never cleans the soul. War only darkens and smears it. For James, the war took away his innocence and he knew that it would never return.

Soon enough, with the months of February ending, the news that James had waited for so long had finally come. On March 16, 1919, an eager Corporal of the United States Army wrote one of his final letters on European soil to let Evelyn know that he was coming home. The March 16th was one of the shortest letters of the entire collection and the final line sums up the general feeling James likely had contained after realizing that he was finally going home.

*St. Germain France*
*March 16th 1919*
*Dear Wife*

*Well the welcome news has arrived at last. We leave this town on our long journey homeward next Wed. morning. I go to Camp*

*Kearney. You will meet me there, cant stop in east. Will wire as soon as we bump into the U.S.A. I cant be still two minutes these days, cant realize am so near to civil life again. These last few months have been so long and weary. Well it will soon be a thing of the past.*

*Semper Fidelis Always faithful*
*Jim.*

James captured his emotions in two short sentences. "These last few months have been so long and weary. Well it will soon be a thing of the past." Since the Armistice was signed on November 11, 1918, James began an internal countdown clock that his potential coming home was becoming a reality. After weeks of disappointed and the prospect of being home for Christmas were shattered, the news of March 16th was one of the greatest moments of his life. Besides the news of the war ending with the Armistice, it was the news that James and Evelyn had been waiting for since he embarked eight months earlier as he began his service in the United States Army.

On March 19, 1919, James Bowman said goodbye to a terrible and horrific chapter of his life. As James left France, it would be the last time he would ever venture outside the United States. James left a part of his soul in the Argonne Forest. When a soldier returns from war, a part of the person needs to be left behind while they begin to reconstruct themselves into civilian life. March 19 is an anniversary for my great-grandfather that he may have never celebrated. It was the anniversary of his restart into normalcy. The last few months of his journey were "long and weary" and soon it became a "thing of the past." Throughout his journey, he remarked that he had hours of stories to tell when he got back to his beloved Evelyn. It is no doubt that many stories of his time on the Western Front were shared but, as time went on, these stories would soon become silent and forgotten. We are left with these letters to re-tell his journey.

Writing the header for the next and final letter was the happiest James had ever been in the last couple of months. It was the first time in nearly nine months since he landed on the shores of Europe that he was finally home. He was free from the uncertainty of waiting and able to send a letter to Evelyn straight from United States soil.

*Camp Upton N.Y.*
*April 5-19*
*My Dearest Sweetheart*

*Just rec'd your letter mailed March 20th this day. Oh at last the censorship is off. I love you-see? You used to scold me for not writing enough love in my letters. I love you-but I am not bashful about it now. Put yourself in the same circumstances – I love you and think of someone you knew and was reading your letters and was around you every day. I love you and see if you could be writing I love you at will. Well I love you-we arrived at New York April 2nd and oh joy it is unspeakable, the air we breathe even is home. I love you.*

*I wired you the 4th. Couldn't get to the office any sooner, I wired to Kit for money, rec'd your letter before leaving France telling me you were badly beaten if not broke and I knew I couldn't reach Sam quick enough so sent to Kit yesterday at 3 P.M. and got the dough this A.M. I love you. I will write her tonight explaining the when fore. I could have wired you the day we arrived but I didnt know what camp we were going to and I wanted to let you know where I was so if for any emergency you wanted to wire me you could so do see? I love you.*

*I am writing this in haste. I am half excited to death over getting this far home. We sailed from St Nazaire France March 25th on the U.S.S. Orizaba and sailed into the golden home waters the early morning of April 2nd. The old Statue of Liberty welcomed us you can bet. I wont attempt to tell how happy a bunch we were at this writing it is unwritable. I will dwell upon it off and on the rest of my natural life. There was 3000 troops aboard mostly 91st. Oh boy what joy. We expect to leave here anytime for Kearny and soon after arriving there we will be out of the Army and you can lay hands upon yours own forever after. I will wire you when we arrive in Kearny and I want you to meet me down there but dont come until I say so as we may not have the privilege of leaving the Camp Area, before being mustered out. I love you.*

*We had good eats on the boat and have had some ever since arriving in Gods Country, in fact my little tummy is sort of rebelling on so much real food all of a sudden. But dont worry dear I can eat some yet, have indulged in ice cream already think of it and had my first piece of pie in almost nine months. Oh how good life is, and wait the best of all yet is to come when I can clamp you in my arms and hold you forever. I can hardly believe it is true yet, maybe I am dreaming. Well I love you, they turned the lights out to have a picture so will close and mail this tonight and write Sunday and give a more thoro demonstration of my happiness,*

*Good night cowgirl, I love you love you love you.*
*Your own little Corporal Jimmm J.A. Bowman*

*Censored by me.*

As James moved on with his life after April 1919, he would never forget the traumatic events of the Meuse Argonne Offensive. James grew frustrated and tired of being a soldier in the events following the Meuse Argonne Offensive. The stalemate of the war caused increased tension and homesickness for James as he was battling to get home and make up for lost time. Even though he was frustrated, James was excited to death to be coming home after nearly a year in the United States Army. James had seen the terrors of war and soon he would be reunited with the love of his life. The final two letters explore the hope that James had for his future. James was looking forward for the first home cook meal in ten months. James was optimistic about the future and what thrills laid ahead when they were finally reunited. James looked forward to the moment, that he would "clamp you in my arms and hold you forever." In the post-Meuse Argonne letters, James planned for their future and predicted many things that never came true. But James delivered on one promise he kept for nearly ten months, never letting Evelyn go.

James signed off on the final letter with "Censored by me," a tongue in check references to the months of military censorship for these private letters. James begins the letter in a sarcastic tone by referencing the countless times Evelyn said that he needed to say I love you more in his letters. In the beginning of each sentence, James begins with an "I love you" for extra measure. But the sign off from James means a little more than a sarcastic playful tone. The last paragraph James writing is filled with intimate expressions of his love for Evelyn. James writes "Oh how good life is and wait the best of all yet is to come when I can clamp you in my arms and hold you forever. I can hardly believe it is true yet, maybe I am dreaming."[118] The only priority James had when he left in July 1918 was to get home to Evelyn and hold her in his arms. Throughout his letters, James referenced the dreams he had of the time he would come back to Evelyn and nothing would ever tear them apart. That dream was finally coming true. This was the final and last remaining letter that James sends home to Evelyn.

---

[118] James A. Bowman, "Letters to Evelyn Bowman" (private possession of Alexander Foy, 2020).

After they were reunited in 1919, James and Evelyn would never separate. For the next forty-nine years, James and Evelyn would have three children and navigate the Great Depression, together as one. They built a family based on blue collar hard-working principles. They would never experience the riches of money but instead the richness of love. They would experience an everlasting bond, where the traumatic events of World War I, only made them stronger instead of striking a divide. James might have fulfilled his promise of discussing the events of the Meuse Argonne Offensive with Evelyn or his two other children, but he would never discuss the events with my grandfather.

When James died in 1972, valuable questions went unanswered. The letters offer a glimpse into his war experience. Like many war letters across the history of the United States, they reveal a unique perspective of men fighting in the depths of hell. Men, during chaos, trying to make sense of the world in which they live. The letters give us a portal into the mind of the thirty-year-old oil worker from a small town, Sandy Lake, Pennsylvania, as he ventured to the muddy, wet fields of France. From the oral histories by my grandfather, James was a complicated man to define. He was shy and quiet and kept to himself. But in these letters, James came alive on the pages. In the letters, James was able to express himself to Evelyn in ways that were difficult to him without a pencil and paper. For the uneducated soldier, the letters served as a sense of healing and connection to a world that was calm and nurturing. Evelyn became a sense of hope and peace for James in a world of chaos. James was able to articulate his experience to Evelyn that no oral history would be able to capture. The letters cannot change history. The letters are a snapshot, forever framed in their time. They allow us access into the war experience that cannot be replicated again. These letters freeze time and allow the shy, reserved soldier to share his story. Through these letters written one hundred years ago, James could tell his story again.

# CHAPTER 4

## WAR AND LEGACY

Most evenings, I would walk with my mother after she returned home from work around 5:15pm. We usually take three laps around the neighborhood and discuss our day. Early on when I was writing this thesis, I was asking many what-if questions as I had researched more about the hardships my great-grandfather endured on the Western Front. As I continued my line of questioning, I came to a thought, "What if my great-grandfather was a murderer?". I posed the question to my mom, who was young, only 14, at the time of his death in 1972. My mom snapped back with tears starting to form in her eyes, "He was not a murderer, he did what he had to do to survive. It was either to kill or be killed. He was fighting for his life." I tried following up with a question, stammering, as I tried to restructure my words to better fit what I was trying to state. But the damage was already done. I had tried to defend my inquiry to determine if my great-grandfather was a killer, but it was too late. "I don't like that word, you didn't know him, he was a kind and gentle man." At that moment, I realized the impact and the power of my words. I realized the impact and importance of this project because I am not dealing with just another public figure, I am dealing with my own family legacy.

The interaction with my mother brought me to the next theme in this story. How do I remember my own history? It has been a question that has been at the back of my mind throughout this process. The concept of memory and history has long been theorized and analyzed amongst historians. Memory is something that is evolving and ever changing, unlike some historical artifacts. For example, the letters and diary of great-grandfather have a concrete place in history that remain relatively unchanged. But how we remember is constantly changing and evolving. The contents of the letters and the diary cannot be changed or altered because they have been written and are permanent. These historical artifacts can be analyzed and critiqued, but their contents remain the same. How we remember the artifacts and the man behind the pencil remains ever changing.

The thesis has three main parts because each piece has had a unique place in re-telling the story of James Bowman. The diary and letters told us about his experience, but this final piece tells us the legacy and the final impact of James on the Bowman family. The legacy of James Bowman can be seen through four main themes: father and son, family and war, the final years, and the everlasting legacy. In the following four themes, I would like to show the connection between James' experience on the Western Front and the life lessons that he brought back from the war to eventually teach his family. The themes address how James continued to be loyal to his family through the very end of his life. The war had given him new perspective on life and James was prepared to share these lessons with his family to help build a better life.

## Father and Son

When I embarked on this project, one of the main reasons for me to write this thesis was to give my grandfather an opportunity to relive special moments with his father. My grandfather is Robert Austin Bowman, the youngest child of James and Evelyn Bowman. He was born in 1930, at the height of the Great Depression, and nearly nine years after his oldest brother James (Jim). My grandfather is the oldest living connection I have with trying to understand James as a father, grandfather, and husband. My grandfather is like James in many ways. He is very quiet, reserved and chooses his words carefully. Also, the fact that every word would be recorded did not help his candor to dive deep into his past and open his emotions. But every short response and delicate maneuvering around the questions gives me more of an understanding of their bond and connection that still lives today with Robert.

Over the past three years, I have conducted various recorded and unrecorded oral histories with my grandfather. I asked him about his relationship with his father, his mother, and his own experience in the US Army. I tried to peel back the layers of the quiet Bowman Boys who have remained steadfast in their belief to use their words wisely for fear of ruffling some feathers. I was focused on building a profile for James Bowman to describe who he was and how he acted but Robert only knew James in the post-war and post-Great Depression phases of his life. It would be hard to understand how James acted before and directly after the war but understanding how he raised his kids gives us an indication on how he moved on from the Meuse Argonne Offensive.

Robert described his father as shy and reserved. "He was shy, very shy, not outgoing, he sort of kept to himself a lot. Minimum of friends, that I can recall, later on there weren't too many...He wouldn't speak up on a lot of conversations, he would just listen."[119] I have asked the same question to describe his father's personality numerous times, always hoping for a different result but my grandfather would use the same three words, shy, reserved, and quiet. As my grandfather described his father, I could not help but pause for a moment and realize that it seems as if Robert would be explaining himself. In large family dinners, you can always find my grandfather at the end of the table, with a red plastic cup filled with box wine, listening. In a way, Robert is describing himself when he talks about the quiet, shy nature of James sitting at a table listening to conversations.

Throughout the interviews, I began to realize that my grandfather had a different relationship with James than his brother and sister. James was nearly forty-three years old when Robert was

[119] Robert Bowman, interview by Alexander Foy, February 27, 2017.

born. By the time Robert was in high school, James was in his mid-fifties. They had a very close relationship towards the end of James's life. Maybe it was the bond of being the youngest child of older siblings, but James and Robert shared a special bond that is hard to explain. The bond between father and son strengthened towards the end of James' life as Robert had become one of the main caretakers to help find the proper nursing homes for James. When I was writing this project, most of my thoughts on James Bowman were also loosely based on my grandfather. James passed on a great amount of his personality to Robert which is why the resemblance of their shy and quiet natures is striking.

When my grandfather described his parents' relationship, he said that "they never fought or seemed angry with each other. They had enjoyed each other's company."[120] They were married for nearly fifty years. When my grandfather read over the letters, I asked him whether it had sounded like how his father would talk to his mother in its delivery and tone. I wanted to know when he read over the letters if he had heard his father's voice again. My grandfather reflected on whether he had heard his father through the diary and

[120] Robert Bowman, interview by Alexander Foy, March 8, 2020.

letters. "I think it was very much him, what he would have written. I believe that knowing him as well as I did."[121] One of the key points in the letters that my grandfather picked up was how James was extremely homesick and lonely as the war dragged on. My grandfather believed his parents' relationship to be very special and that "his loneliness and being away from his wife, it had sounded like the way he would have been. It was the way he wrote about her and the way he missed her."[122] My grandfather looked back at his relationship with his parents with much fondness and appreciation. He had maintained a close and steady relationship with his parents and looked after both of his parents in the later portions of their lives.

After reading the letters, my grandfather also learned something new from his father. The one surprise in the letters and diary was James' need for some "good ole American candy." James mentioned numerous times to Evelyn that whenever she sent letters to include some American candy. Whenever James would receive payroll, he would save some extra cash to buy some chocolate or

---

[121] Robert Bowman, interview by Alexander Foy, March 8, 2020.

[122] Robert Bowman, interview by Alexander Foy, March 8, 2020.

take an opportunity to trade some belongings for some candy. The letters with the candy had surprised my grandfather because "he doesn't remember him being a candy eater. That was kind of surprising."[123] The letters had given Robert new perspective on how his father changed over the post war years. As my grandfather grew up, he noticed that his father was never much of a candy eater. James had changed even after his post war years to move away from candy as he began to age. The letters gave Robert another opportunity to revisit a part of his father's life and recount some of the fond memories of his father. It was an opportunity for him to hear his father's voice again and to connect with a man that has been gone for forty-eight years.

Robert learned many life lessons from James as he grew up in Long Beach, California. It could have been the bond of being the youngest siblings that brought them together or the connection of being the quietest people in the room. As Robert entered adulthood, the father and son would face be connected through another shared experience; being drafted into the United States Army.

## War and Family

---

[123] Robert Bowman, interview by Alexander Foy, March 8, 2020.

James was not the last of the Bowman boys to be called into service for the United States. History would call the next two sons into war as the United States fought in World War II and the Korean War. Jim was drafted into the United States Navy, serving on a PT boat in the Pacific during World War II. Robert was drafted into the United States Army, serving as an aviation engineer at Fort Huachuca in southern Arizona, during the Korean War. The Bowman boys each had their place in the United States military during world conflict. With each Bowman boy taking part in the military, they each had different and unique experiences that allowed me to look through a lens on the impact of war on the Bowman family.

*Figure 9*: Corporal Robert A. Bowman.

James did not share his war experiences with my grandfather. Robert believes that James could have shared some of the small details of his time on the Meuse Argonne Offensive, but it is unsure if he ever did disclose what happened in the Argonne Forest. When it came time for the United States government to call upon the Bowman Boys, the experience in the Great War had prepared the family for these world conflicts. James and Evelyn had already been through the fear and anxiety of a draft notice coming through the mail so they were prepared for what would come next for their two draft eligible sons.

When the draft notice came in the mail to the Bowman home on 20th Street in Long Beach, it was calling for the youngest of the Bowman children. By the time the draft notice arrived at the home in early 1952, the Bowman family had already withstood the emotional toll of sending two family members. During this time of great anxiety, Robert does not recall any comments that his parents made for getting the draft notice. "I don't remember a comment. I'm sure he was concerned about it. But I don't really remember what he had said."[124] When I followed up with him, he believes that "they figured I was going to get it. They never said anything about it. It wasn't anything verbal that I can recall."[125] But maybe this lapse of memory and old age of my grandfather gives a detail on how James and Evelyn had dealt with another family member going to war. The quiet and shy couple dealt with the draft notice of their youngest son the only way they knew how, to accept the fact and move on. Just like James in World War I and Jim in World War II, the Bowmans accepted the call of the United States and did what they were told. Whether they had any reservations or objections, they suited up and followed orders. It is a mentality that has stuck with the family well beyond their time in the United States military.

As my grandfather recalled his time in the United States military, I found that his experience was much different than his father's. My grandfather never served overseas and stayed on United States soil for his entire two years of military service. It must have been a blessing for James and Evelyn to know that their son was going to be safe and sound in the United States and away from

---

[124] Robert Bowman, interviewed by Alexander Foy, November 14, 2017.

[125] Robert Bowman, interviewed by Alexander Foy, March 8, 2020.

enemy forces overseas. But, as my grandfather shared the details of his time in the United States military, there was one question I did not ask. It has been a question that has been the elephant in the room for nearly sixty-six years since he disembarked from Fort Huachuca in February of 1954. "Why does he still believe he didn't 'serve'?" It is a question that my family has been trying to convince my grandfather every time he disagrees. He has given his reasoning over the years and the one that usually sticks are that he believes that "I didn't go overseas, and I don't think it's right to take shine away from the guys that did."

The most vivid moment of this was at Christmas when I had purchased a brick for him at the World War I Memorial and Museum in Kansas City. A year before, I had purchased a brick for his father and for the upcoming Christmas season, my family decided to buy one for him. My mom prepped the gift in her usual ways by saying that the gift was "from all of us grandkids and kids" but it was a joint idea of my mother and myself. When my grandfather had opened the gift, he looked directly at me. There was nothing my mom could say to lead my grandfather to believe that the gift was from anyone else. But what happened after the gift is important because it highlighted an issue that has haunted my grandfather since 1954. After saying his initial thank you, the second comment was no surprise to me but much to the chagrin of my mom and grandmother. Without missing any moment to let the room fall into silence, my grandfather says, "this is very nice, but I did not go overseas." And just like my grandfather, my mother and grandmother did not miss a beat to push out that negativity by piling on with "yes, you did, dad" and "stop it, you served." This was not the first moment my grandmother and mother jumped on him for saying that he did not serve. In one of the earliest oral interviews, my grandmother, playing Solitaire on the computer, stopped her game to interpret my grandfather to remind him that he did serve, and he should stop it.[126] There have been numerous times that these interactions have happened with my grandfather and my family and they all end up the same way: my grandfather makes his comment on why he didn't serve and the hot headed Italians in my family quickly shoot him down.

In these interactions, I have noticed more than just a common annoyance my family has with my grandfather coming to terms with accepting his time in the military. In each of these interactions, I

[126] Robert Bowman, interviewed by Alexander Foy, February 27, 2017.

have noticed something deeper with my grandfather. It is a sense of guilt. It is a shame of not partaking in the mission overseas and being stuck in the United States. My grandfather received a medical deferment for having flat feet as the main reason for why he stayed on American soil (Fort Ord and Fort Huachuca) instead of Korea. My grandfather has never volunteered to share information about his time in the military outside of oral interviews. He has made it to the point where he has kept it hidden and rarely shares his experience with others in a feeling of guilt.

My grandfather has never attended veteran meetings, joined associations, or wore Korean War or Infantry designated hats. Whenever we would go on a cruise, I would joke around and tell him he should go to Veteran meetups, but he would always dismiss that notion with "I don't have anything in common with them." In an indirect way, my grandfather speaks with his actions. He expresses his emotions regarding being a homebody soldier through these denials or fear of a stolen valor through these subtle actions.

I have tried to analyze why my grandfather feels guilty about serving in the war. I feel as if he has a deeper guilt for some other reason, but it is a feeling that he will never truly share. James was like his son in this aspect. Like James, my grandfather rarely shares his feelings and the true meaning behind how he felt regarding his time in the United States Army. My grandfather could feel a guilt because he never lived up to his father's legacy in the war. But I do not believe that to be the case. I believe that my grandfather feels guilty for staying in the United States while countless men that he trained with at Fort Ord were loaded into trucks to be eventually shipped out to Korea. He has been dealing with the fact that his life was drastically changed when he received word that he was not leaving. It could be a form of survivor's guilt.

Veterans that stayed on American soil have this similar feeling of survivor's guilt. In the fallout of 9/11, United States Marines often had a similar feeling of guilt of staying put in the United States while their comrades fought overseas. One Marine shares a similar experience of having to relive the guilt every time he discusses his time in the United States military. "It's always hard for me to tell people I wasn't deployed. Conversations usually end up with "so what did you do then?" as if I had no purpose in the military if I wasn't deployed."[127] These conversations can be difficult for those that undergo the grueling task of basic training, advance to specialized training, and then prepare to be deployed just to be reassigned to a different base. The sense of being reassigned while your fellow service members board a plane to your targeted destination creates this deep-seated guilt. As another interviewed Marine said, "I wanted to fight, not to earn a badge of honor or a ribbon. It was the job I trained for."[128] The guilt of staying home can wear away the fact that you served in the United States military to assist the overall goal of their mission. Without engineers, no machines are built. Without payroll, no one gets paid. Each position has a role that needs to be executed for the success of the overall mission.

[127] Katie Connelly, "Frustration for the US soldiers who never went to war," BBC News, BBC, July 10, 2010, accessed on March 8, 2020, https://www.bbc.com/news/world-us-canada-10547610.

[128] Katie Connelly, "Frustration for the US soldiers who never went to war," BBC News, BBC, July 10, 2010, accessed on March 8, 2020, https://www.bbc.com/news/world-us-canada-10547610.

*Figure 10*: Corporal Robert A. Bowman at Fort Huachuca.

As my grandfather had undergone basic training, he had built up a sense of camaraderie with his fellow soldiers. He said that nearly half the men he trained with at Fort Ord went over in some capacity to fight in Korea. My grandfather was grouped with those who had medical deferments which included men who were overweight and had other physical deformities. My grandfather was in great physical condition, but the military concern about flat feet at the time stopped him from being deployed. Flat feet, also known as pes planus, was a condition where the feet have a flat longitudinal arch that comes into nearly complete contact with the floor when standing.[129] During World War II and the Korean War, flat feet were seen as a deformity and those men would be plagued with pain and injury. One major attribute to the flat feet myth was the lack of scientific testing. Dr. Francesca Thompson, former chief of the orthopedic adult foot clinic at Roosevelt Hospital in New York remarked, "we've all been brought up on grandmother's warning that flat feet are bad, so we'd better correct them. As we've become more scientific, we've begun to ask, 'why?'"[130] Studies have shown that flat feet no longer offer any structural or biomechanical limitations under current military physical requirements.[131] Even with this medical deferment, staying home made my grandfather feel a sense of guilt that he had to live out the rest of his military service in the desert rather than the frontlines.

My grandfather can find some sense of peace in staying home during the Korean War. In early 1954, when he was on leave, he met a girl at a bowling alley near Belmont Shore. With a giant

---

129 R. Buchbinder. 2004. Plantar Fasciitis. The New England Journal of Medicine. Vol. 350.

130 Elisabeth Rosenthal. 1990. "The Maligned Flat Foot: Some See an Advantage." *New York Times (1923-Current File)*, 1990. http://search.proquest.com/docview/108456559/.

131 Ann Lurati. 2015. "Flat Feet and a Diagnosis of Plantar Fasciitis in a Marine Corps Recruit." *Workplace Health & Safety* 63 (4): 136–38. https://doi.org/10.1177/2165079915576923.

clock on the wall, he asked her if she had the time. Fast forward sixty-six years later, three kids, and six grandchildren, I think that his life turned out well considering the circumstances.

For my grandfather, the military had taught him disciple in his life. My grandfather went into the workforce with the same attitude he had in the Army. He was always a general laborer, following orders of management and never really taking on responsibility. As he was once said in an oral interview, "I never wanted to get promoted because I didn't want to take the headaches home."[132] He liked following rules and did what needed to be done in order to accomplish the goal for the day. He was married a few months after he was discharged from the Army. Even in his marriage, he still could not kick a small habit of Army life. In the U.S. Army, he was taught to hang his clothes facing left, which meant that the buttons would face the left side of the closet. Years into his marriage, he had kept this discipline that he learned in the Army until my grandmother kept moving them and he slowly gave up on facing his clothes to the left.

---

[132] Robert Bowman, interviewed by Alexander Foy, November 14, 2017.

My grandfather is a hero. He has taught me so many life lessons through his actions. He rarely had some long speech about why you should act a certain way; instead, he modeled the way. He did not need to see action to serve his country to become a hero. He became a hero as a civilian. He taught his children to be fair, to respect each other, and to always care for their family. He instilled a creed and a way of life through his actions. Like James, Robert had built a family on core values of the golden rule, "treat others as you want to be treated." He wanted to show his family that your actions reflect your character. If you treat others with respect, then you will live a healthy, happy, and fulfilling life.

Like his father and brother, he followed orders and went where the United States military needed them. No matter how much he wants to brood over the fact that he never went overseas, the decisions that were made by United States Army officials were out of his hands. He was ordered to stay and work on valuable air aviation engineering projects at Fort Huachuca that would help the relatively new military branch, United States Air Force. The guilt was always there for my grandfather, but he obeyed orders and accomplished the job he had set out to do. Like his father and brother, no matter the role, the Bowman Boys did what they were assigned to do. A lesson that they had taught each other as a pillar of life. James would continue to teach life lessons through his actions. James believed in taking care of his family and continued this even as his health began to deteriorate even in the final years of his life.

## The Final Years

In the late 1960s, Evelyn suffered a stroke that left her dependent on outside care. James was focused on taking care of her by himself. Robert described it as "a nervous breakdown." The doctors then began to start shock treatments, but the problem continued to worsen. The doctors had diagnosed Evelyn with a disease related to Parkinson's and potentially a form of ALS. In his late 70s, James' sole focus was to keep them together and away from the fear of being split up in a nursing home. But as the disease started to attack Evelyn's body, it had gotten worse where she could no longer speak or swallow. One day Robert received a phone call. "My dad called me at work, and he couldn't wake her up, so I immediately went over, she had had a stroke, we figured later. We had to call an ambulance and they took her to the hospital."[133] The

[133] Robert Bowman, interviewed by Alexander Foy, November 14, 2017.

following day, Evelyn Bowman had passed away. The latter part of her life made it very difficult for James to take care of Evelyn. Robert observed his parent's relationship as it began to approach the final years of their lives. "My father had to take care of her the best he could."[134]

In the aftermath of the Meuse Argonne Offensive, James wrote a promise in the diary that he would fulfill forty years later. "It is to you Evelyn that I owe all these riches you showed me the open door and helped me in. I owe a debt to you I can never fully repay but by jinks. I'll keep at it and if love will ever pay the bill, I can pay quite a heap of it in time."[135] James kept a promise to repay the debt of having to withstand the anxiety of war. It was a promise that was "sewed" each day since he returned from the Western Front. He built that promise through his actions by caring and providing for his family.

With his care for Evelyn ending, the death had hit James very hard. He had traveled to live with Jim up in Bakersfield and eventually back down to Long Beach to live with his daughter,

---

[134] Robert Bowman, interviewed by Alexander Foy, November 14, 2017.

[135] James A. Bowman. *Diary, 1918-1919.* Transcribed by Cheryl Foy and Alexander Foy.

Betty. When he stayed with Betty, he began to lose his memory and soon it became a "little difficult for her to take care of him there so she had him put into this nursing home in Cherry Avenue in Long Beach."[136] Although it was not diagnosed, James began to display early stages of Alzheimer's. In the Long Beach nursing home, he would start talking about when he was a kid back in Pennsylvania. Even though his mind was regressing, he still shared some of his earliest memories as a kid. Robert would say, "I used to go over there, and he didn't know who I was. I had to explain it and finally it would come to him and it just got worse and worse."[137]

James was placed at the same nursing home as his brother, Uncle Sam. But as his mind began to deteriorate, so did the patience of those handling James. Uncle Sam called Robert and asked if they could move him to another nursing home. Uncle Sam did not know what to do with him while he was there, so Robert made the decision to move him again. As James moved to the next nursing home, it became very clear that James's health was worsening.

> I was working at Westinghouse and I used to stop in on a night shift, I used to stop in before I would go to work to see

---

[136] Robert Bowman, interviewed by Alexander Foy, November 14, 2017.

[137] Robert Bowman, interviewed by Alexander Foy, November 14, 2017.

> how he was doing which he didn't know who I was. I would talk to him there and my brother came down to see him there and he...It was just hard for us because you know he didn't know who we were then finally. I went to stop by one time and the nurse said, we had to take him away in an ambulance and they never called me and then they said, so then I went to the hospital and he was there, and he had a stroke, eventually, he was mumbling a lot, he was in a room with about three other people.[138]

I asked my grandfather what it was like talking to him and having him not knowing who you are. In one of the most candid responses of the interview, my grandfather answered straight and with emotion. No longer calculated and speaking as if he was reliving the final days of his father's life.

> That's very difficult because you want him to know that you're there supporting him and everything you know, "I'm Bob, your son" and "I'm Jim, your son" and just not registering and that was hard. Of course, he felt no pain, I guess. You know, he would speak, you know, it wasn't like he couldn't talk. He just didn't know who we were that's like I said it slowly started when he first left my sister's in the place in Long Beach there and I would go in and finally realize who I was but then as time went on and a couple of new, different places, we had to take him to he just got to that way were he didn't know where he was [in the nursing home]. That was difficult [for us].[139]

My grandfather never elaborated on his father's death past what he said in the interview. I never pressed him to tell me how he

---

[138] Robert Bowman, interviewed by Alexander Foy, November 14, 2017.

[139] Robert Bowman, interviewed by Alexander Foy, November 14, 2017.

felt in the moment when his father was slowly losing his memory and could no longer recognize his son. I know that my grandfather does not like displaying his emotions too much. I know that the moment of losing a parent is very difficult and reliving that moment can open a wound all over again. James passed away, surrounded by his son, Robert, and daughter-in-law, on March 4, 1972.

The later part of James's life is important in the context of his story because it is a testament to who he was as a person. He cared for his family. He might not have been the loudest in the room, but you knew through actions that he cared. James was faithful to his God, his wife, and his family. In the hardest times of his life, James relied on Evelyn for support. Through the bullets of Meuse Argonne and the unemployment lines of the Great Depression, James had Evelyn and Evelyn had James. They were connected to each other from the moment he arrived back from the Western Front. James relied on Evelyn for support while he was thousands of miles away in the fields of the Argonne Forest. In his letters, he talked about the great future ahead and how he was always going to cherish her each moment.

James remained faithful to Evelyn to the very end. When Robert searched for nursing homes that would keep them together, James did not listen. He could not stand the thought of going into a home and getting separated from his love. Robert tried and pleaded but James remained loyal to the fact that it was his duty to take care of Evelyn.

> I checked around and my dad never wanted to put her some place and be separated so I checked around to different places and I found out there were a lot of different places they could go together, and the social security would handle it you know for both of them. And I said, "Dad, I found a place, places where we could go and we could give mom, they could take care of her and you, and you'd be in the same place, same room". He wouldn't go for it. He just, "Na, I didn't believe it, they'll separate us". I said, "No, they wouldn't do that, I checked." I couldn't talk him into it. It would have made it easier for him, if they would have bathed her and stuff and he would have to take her into the bathroom and stuff and that would have all been handled but he would not go for it and I tried but it was tough.[140]

Ever since the war separated them in 1918, James was not going to let anything separate them and he kept his promise even through the last years of their time together. Even though it accelerated the decline of his own health, it was a noble and loving act for James to sacrifice his energy to care for Evelyn. They had only known each

---

[140] Robert Bowman, interviewed by Alexander Foy, November 14, 2017.

other a few short months before he left for the Western Front. A stray bullet or a grenade blast could have drastically changed their lives and the course of history for the countless families that were started because of their marriage. They were soul mates, connected by a love so deep that no words can describe it. Any attempt on my part will not do it justice.

## Everlasting Legacy

In the past three chapters, I have written about my great-grandfather's diary, letters, and the impact James has had on my grandfather. I wanted to write about the importance that this project had in preserving my family's history so future generations can read about the hardships and triumphs of James Bowman. I wanted to write about the connection between a father and a son, connection between two wars, and an unwritten family legacy that carries on today. When writing this thesis, I have always tried to have an answer for one simple question: "what is this telling me?" I have examined his letters, diary, and his family relationships. I have done months of research on books, pictures, articles, and family artifacts, all on how they connect to my great-grandfather's story. But the last part of this research that I have left unexamined is my relationship to a man that I never met.

In the beginning of this thesis, I wanted to construct a profile of my great-grandfather. I wanted to gather all the information and data available to piece him together. From the pictures to the letters to the oral interviews from my grandfather, I wanted to create a physical and mental profile where I could begin to connect to a man I had never met. As I was constructing this profile, I began to place myself in his shoes. I began to think about how he felt, what he saw and how this experience changed him. It was a way I could connect to him. When I began writing the first two chapters of this thesis, I was left with more unanswered questions. I was left with the same response from my grandfather, "He never shared that part of his life." I wanted to expand what was in the diary. I wanted to have the opportunity to ask my great-grandfather, what did he mean by that. But from these unanswered questions, I was able to focus on what was right in front of me. Instead of focusing on what could not be answered, I narrowed down to the concrete examples of what James Bowman left. The diary and the letters were an opportunity to retrace the steps and open his life again. By placing myself in his shoes, I was able to connect to my great-grandfather in ways I would have never imagined. I was able to give him a platform to retell his own story. After a century, the quiet and shy Bowman was able to speak again.

As I began to write about my great-grandfather's experience, I realized that there was a connection with what he was writing to how my family has formed connections. The one selection in the diary that resonated the most to me was when my great-grandfather wrote in the fallout of the Meuse Argonne Offensive about how he will teach his children. "My children shall be taught Patriotisms as a sort of religion as long as the stars and stripes continue to wave in the just and righteous cause it now stands for. It has never been stained with dishonor and man be unto the man that dares to degrade it."[141] The passage resonates with me because it begins to make me evaluate how I view the world and the pride I have for the United States. My family has been rooted in a blue-collar mentality and even when families are combined in marriage, the mentality continues to live on. The blue-collar mentality is an important aspect of how we have shaped our worldview. The United States has gotten

[141] James A. Bowman. *Diary, 1918-1919.* Transcribed by Cheryl Foy and Alexander Foy.

itself into a fair share of controversial situations both home and abroad. But my family has had an optimistic approach to how we view the direction of the country.

As I reflect on my worldview, I seem to connect to the one-hundred-year-old viewpoint of my great-grandfather. I believe that the United States is a strong country. There is no denying the fact that we have our issues. I believe that my worldview has been shaped from my family and the pride that we have in our country. My family has rarely had a leadership role in their professional lives and have never rose to the level of manager. We have always had a mindset of a blue-collar outlook towards any situation. The blue-collar outlook can be found in our viewpoint of how we see the United States. My family views the United States as part of a team, when you lose, you regroup, when you win, you celebrate. I believe that this patriotic outlook began with my great-grandfather. But my great-grandfather answered the call, like many other brave Americans, to assist the Allied troops in Europe. There were moments in my great-grandfather's experience where he did not want to be on the Western Front, but he knew that he owed it to his country to fight and try to end the war. My great-grandfather had the patriotic goal in mind when trying to end this fight. He saw it through the lens of clarity, we defeat the enemy, then we could go home, I will be happy, and I can move on with my life. The patriotic viewpoint of my family grew from my great-grandfather's willingness to risk his life for the betterment of the United States. It is a pride in the country that allows us to have an optimistic viewpoint of the United States.

My connection with my great-grandfather is much deeper than the letters and diary. It is a way of life that has been passed down from generation to generation. James was the quietest man in the room. A piece of this personality that is found in my grandfather, my mother, and myself. This way of life has been taught through letting your actions speak volumes and to choose your words carefully. It is something that I have learned from the countless family dinners, lunches, and gatherings at my grandparents' house. As we sit in the patio room with one long table, my grandfather sits in the back corner. He talks to the people around him, only asking questions. But, mostly, he is listening. Listening, observing, and picking up what other people have to say. It is something that his father did. Sitting at the table and listening. My family has its set of eccentric characters. We have our people that will fill up the moments of silence with more conversations and repeat the same story they told last month. From the over twenty-five years of family gatherings, I have done the same thing: sitting, listening, and observing. It seems like such a miniscule example of a family tradition, but it is simply more than that. Like iron ore being cast into steel, the quiet, reflective nature of my family has been forged for nearly a century. It is a way of life that has been hardened by events and through adversity and grit. It is the connection of this quiet and reflective nature that has been transferred between my great-grandfather, grandfather, and myself.

Through my grandfather's quiet nature at the dinner table, I can see that James' legacy is still alive today. Because his legacy is not stuck in a shoebox, only to be taken out occasionally, but it is found in the actions of his family. In a way, my family is a walking reflection of his diary in World War I. In the diary, James writes about his hopes and dreams of what he will teach his kids when they grow up. He wrote a promise to Evelyn and to his future family that he was going to teach them a good way to live. On the Western Front, James never knew what the next day would bring so he had time to think about what he would do when he returned. James did not squander this opportunity to teach his kids the value of respect, determination, and grit. Like the passing of the guard, my grandfather took the lessons that he learned from his father and taught them to my mother and subsequently my mother had passed these qualities to me.

The most valuable lesson I learned from reexamining the story of James Bowman is to always be dependable for your family even during the hardest times. When my great-grandfather moved across the country for new opportunity, he only had his brother, Uncle Sam, to rely on. When James entered the war, he had to rely on my great-grandmother for support in the form of a letter that came from thousands of miles away. When the Great Depression hit, the family had to rely on each other to make it through one of the hardest economic times in the country's history. When Evelyn's health was declining, she had to rely on James, in his late seventies, to sacrifice his health to take care of his love in the last years of her life. For when James began his decline, he had to rely on his son, Robert, to financially support him as he sought the professional care needed to improve James's quality of life. It is a family tradition of being dependable in the hardest of times. It is sacrificing your happiness, well-being, and energy to make sure that your loved ones can have a better quality of life. It is looking out for the betterment of the family even if you must sacrifice your personal goals or dreams. It is a family tradition that is built with doing what needs to be done. My family has sacrificed a lot for each other, helping each other to accomplish their goals and live happy and healthy lives. That is the lesson I can take away by reflecting on my great-grandfather's journey. He did what he had to do in order to help his comrades on the Western Front, his country, and his family. He learned how to make sacrifices for others, even in the most turbulent times, which is a lesson that he taught his family. A lesson that I have learned from my grandfather and mother. A lesson that I hope to pass on to my own family. A lesson of making personal sacrifices of your own goals and dreams so that you can help others achieve their success.

# CHAPTER 5

## CONCLUSION

Nearly one hundred years ago, my great-grandfather's journey began as he boarded a train headed for the Western Front. His mind was filled with nervousness and doubt about the unknown. He had traveled, mostly on foot, through the forests and countryside of France to fight men who were dubbed the enemy of the United States. Along the way, he recorded his thoughts, dreams, and anxieties about what lay ahead in the unforeseeable future. He wrote letters that filled the entire page to his newly married wife over three thousand miles away. He, along with one million other American men, charged through the barren forests of the Argonne. Withstanding machine gun fire, he navigated his way through the small French village of Epinonville and met the German troops. He, along with other members of the 364$^{th}$ Infantry, had as the citation wrote an "aggressiveness and willingness to close with the enemy, and an indifference to machine gun fire."[142] He was promoted to Corporal following the Meuse Argonne Offensive by his example of high conduct for which he was subsequently promoted.[143] He traveled to Belgium and waited for four months for word to be sent home. In mid-March, he began his journey home to the country he fought to defend. For the next fifty years, he would raise a family, survive the Great Depression, and live out the rest of his life with his "Dearest Sweetheart" by his side.

The diary and letters are an important historical document for my family. They not only give my family the opportunity to reexamine my great-grandfather's journey throughout the Western Front, but they are also a credit to how my family has preserved family history. For years, my family has preached the importance of keeping family heirlooms and have organized these heirlooms by family (Bowman and Cipriani). It is a testament to my family for keeping this diary and letters safe for over one hundred years. One fatal spring cleaning or one garage sale could have lost the diaries

---

[142] Citation from 91st Division. United States Army. (Private collection of Alexander Foy, 2020).

[143] Citation from 91st Division. United States Army. (Private collection of Alexander Foy, 2020).

and letters forever. The diary and letters have had a strange journey to end up in my possession. They were kept in safe keeping for over one hundred years. They endured moves from apartments to homes multiple times and a passage down to their children. My grandfather was one of three children that could have gotten these letters and they very well could have ended up in the hands of my great-uncle and great-aunt, who are now both deceased. The diary and letters were on a journey like my great-grandfather as he navigated the Great War.

I refer to his diary and letters as a journey because I truly believe that James Bowman never finished his journey one-hundred years ago. I believe that James's story was never finished when he boarded that ship to come back to the United States in March 1919. A story is told twice, once as it unfolds and the other as it is re-told again. My great-grandfather had the opportunity to reflect on his experience on the Western Front and gave me the opportunity to retell it again in a different form. I have noted many times throughout this thesis that my great-grandfather was a shy and quiet man. He had the opportunity to share his experience with his sons but chose to keep those events private and locked away. I will never know if my great-grandfather experienced any form of PTSD from the war which pushed him to remain silent for the rest of his life, never to speak about the war again. Life has a unique way of unfolding. James may have censored the true story of his experience but through his silence gave me an opportunity to retell his story through my eyes. I was able to discover and connect to my great-grandfather in a different way than hanging a picture on the wall. I was able to retrace his steps through the Meuse Argonne Offensive and understand the hardships of war with the new advancements of machine guns, airplanes, and other new industrialized tools of warfare. Like my great-grandfather, I was on a journey to revisit his past that has been silent for so many years.

In the mix of the forty-three letters, one lone letter stood out. It was different in handwriting and the signature at the bottom. It was addressed nearly three months before James entrained in Camp Lewis, Washington headed to the east coast. It is the only one of its kind in this collection and so far, is the only surviving letter that Evelyn wrote to James during his time in the United States Army. The letter was addressed March 18, 1918, at the time when James had left the valley of Kern County to the forest of upper Washington.

James was possibly in basic training and gearing up for the escalation of World War I. In March 1918, the Germans had launched the only attempt to salvage the war in the shape of the Ludendorff Offensive. The Russians had bowed out of the war by this time and soon it would only be the United States to aid the Allies of Europe in hopes of bringing the stalemate of the Great War to a bitter end. The letter is the only glimpse of Evelyn's writing style and how Evelyn would converse with James through written communication.

*Tacoma Wash*
*Mar. 18. 1918*

*My dearest Love*

*I know wont receive any letter tomorrow but will write one anyway just to keep on the good side of you isn't that right dear? Pat and her girlfriend came in on the three o'clock bus. Pat wanted me to meet her. So I stayed down with the girls. I've went to three shows, to pass the time away her girlfriend went home and Edith was down to the boat with Mr. Hill. Mr Hill was at the bus last night. Ask all about the quarantine. He knew that I was going home on that bus because he had seen Edith and Clyde that afternoon. I cant believe pleasure he gets out of just seeing me for a minute.*

*The show made me cry. The two people in it could be in love with each other it made me homesick for you dear because they were just like us. Loved with the very deepest of love. Oh! dearie love. The times seemed so short while you were in. (Censored) when you leave it seems like everything is gone, but I was glad to have you home for a short time anyway but I always feel lonely and blue after you leave me. There is a big space there that I cant explain when you are not* *near me but no one else can take its place. I receive the $35. this morning I wonder why Sam doesnt write I wonder if he is mad at me?*

*Now dear I think you are mistaken about me weakening in its smoking proposition. I cant remember of it unless you mean the time I got mad and handed you the cigarettes. I was trying you dear to see what sort of a man you were, if you had smoked one I wouldn't be where I am today. And another time I remember I ask you if I was really depriving you of something that you needed by not letting you smoke. Everyone said that a fellow needed it while in the Army. Of course I cant see it that way, but I thought this way. I love you so very much. I didnt want to deprive you of something you really needed, and dear have I explained it now? If at anytime one thing like that would save your life, forget me. I will know you didnt do it because you wanted it. I wanted you to have all that you needed in this Army life to make you comfortable and if you really could to smoke I wasnt going to stand in your way see dear? Somehow it doesn't seem that you ever smoked to me. I guess because I had never seen you do it.*

*I saw Mr Marvin last night as far as I know now will be out Tues night if it doesnt rain but dear you remember I will leave here about one as that is the only time I can get in. So if it rains after that you will know that I am on my way. Well no I cant say that I will say that. I will leave town about 3.30 if it isn't raining at that time see. It wont hurt tho to take a run over to the Hosters House because I am able to come anyway. Mr Marvin said he would come clear out to get me but I dont want him to do that unless Connie comes with him. She will think I am trying to steal him. Pat and I had quite an argument last night. Marvin gives Connie five and six dollars pr's of hose all the time gives her gloves, etc. I say it isnt right. But Pat thinks it is alright. She says it is just as bad to accept candy and flowers. I say not I think wearing apparel is wrong to give to a girl. Am I not right dear? My mother would never let me do it I guess that is the reason I look at it that way. I didnt notice that you spelt quarantine wrong I look on some of your letters and it was right, have I been spelling it right wrong. I mean it is 11.30 wont get this tomorrow if I dont close. So I love you very much.*

*Your sweetheart Eve*[144]

In his diary, James had written copy of an unknown letter from Evelyn in the July 12th entry. But this is the lone letter that is the only surviving physical letter in existence from Evelyn during their communication in World War I. The lone letter offers a unique perspective for this project because it challenged me to stay grounded in the evidence that my great-grandfather presented. Throughout this project, I always wondered the what if. What happened? What did he mean? I read into everything. I tried to write to the what-if. The lone letter is an important reminder to the research of my project. It is a reminder that we cannot always worry about the information that we do not have. I stressed about the information and the stories that James never shared. I developed a regret to my great-grandparents for never recording their stories, so I was able to cherish them for this moment. I wanted to evaluate the experience of James by building something that may have never happened.

---

[144] Bowman, Evelyn, "Letter to James Bowman (1918)", transcribed by Cheryl Foy. (Private collection of Alexander Foy, 2020). Letter is transcribed as written with all spelling and grammatical mistakes.

The lone letter reminded me to appreciate the information that I possessed instead of paying attention to what is not said. The thesis was built upon information that my family held onto for over one hundred years. The thesis taught me a lesson in the preservation of history. The lesson was to stop looking for things that do not exist and to look for what is right in front of you. Once I was able to realize this valuable lesson, it allowed me to guide James to tell his story. Through this thesis, I was able to give him a mouthpiece to re-tell his story through the words he wrote one hundred years ago and not the made-up words and themes by his great-grandson.

If history ever repeats itself, Evelyn's letters may appear again in the future. But if they do not, I am still fortunate for the information that I do possess and the opportunity to bring my great-grandfather's one-hundred-year-old story alive again. Through the letters and the diary, I was able to give my great-grandfather a voice that was silent for so long. I believe that this thesis was a responsibility that I owed to my family. I believe that collective effort of my grandparents to cherish the diary and letters of James Bowman, afforded me the opportunity to bring his story to light. I was able to be the guide for the man that my grandfather and mother admired the most. It is a tremendous amount of pressure to write about your family in an objective way.

The absence of these stories that James never shared were a great burden on me earlier in the thesis. I developed an underlying resentment that he never wrote anything more down that I could use. Even in the diary, he remarked that he was going to add on to his war stories. But he only left behind his letters and diary, which was more than enough to bring the story to life. I am grateful for the opportunity to tell his story through his own words. I am fortunate that I was able to preserve my family history so that my own children can read about a shy and brave man as he navigated the dark, cruel world of war. I am proud that I was able to piece together my great-grandfather's story.

As I wrap up this thesis, I find it important to reflect on the nature of my work as a historian. I can think back to my time in fifth grade where I fell in love with researching history. Whether it was researching baseball, indigenous people, the Civil War, or the Apollo mission, I can remember being fascinated with the process of learning how events developed. I carried this fascination with history into high school and eventually college where I was interested in capturing stories. Whenever I would share with other people that I was a history major, I would always get the same two responses. A puzzled look of "why would you major in history" and "I loved history in high school, but it can be boring." I always felt as if I had to defend myself on the importance of history because like most majors, the field is everchanging. To those that believe history is boring, they have compacted it into a bunch of useless dates that they must memorize for a test. For me, history is about capturing stories. It is about how we have developed over time as people. It is about the art of capturing stories and preserving what happened in the past so that it can hopefully teach us something about the present.

In 2018, the Great War marked its one-hundred-year anniversary since the Armistice Day on November 11, 1918. When I embarked on this thesis, I always thought World War I was the forgotten war to World War II that followed twenty-one years later. In American public memory, World War II has always been the more fascinating and illustrious war for us to study and research. The cause for which we fought seems to be more heroic in World War II (ending the Nazis and revenge against the Japanese Empire) than

World War I (helping the British and French). Those that fought in World War II were defined in American culture as "the Greatest Generation" while those in World War I came back to a failed veteran benefit system. With the one-hundred-year anniversary, it has brought back to light the stories of World War I. In recent years, the stories of World War I have come to light with the films by Peter Jackson (*They Shall Not Grow Old*) and Sam Mendes (*1917*). In 2019, two separate World War I diaries and items were found in a Leicestershire barn and another diary was sold at auction.[145] These new discoveries and films, allow a new generation to explore the Great War through a new lens. It helps continue the ongoing dialogue of how we preserve the history of the past, especially, when all these men and women involved with the conflict have passed

---

[145] Items of Lt. Stuart Leslie were found in a Leicestershire barn. Items included flying log book, rolls of gun camera photographs and aerial maps that would have been on his knee in the cockpit of the plane. The collection was sold at auction. ("WW1 pilot's items found in Leicestershire barn 'flabbergasts' expert," BBC News, BBC, February 19, 2020, accessed on March 19, 2020, https://www.bbc.com/news/uk-england-leicestershire-51558511.)

The diary of Angus McKenzie Forsyth, a Military Cross honorary from Nottingham, was auctioned off in December 2019. ("Nottingham soldier's war diary goes under the hammer," BBC News, BBC, December 12, 2019, accessed on March 19, 2020, https://www.bbc.com/news/uk-england-nottinghamshire-50758400.)

A diary of Pvt. Arthur Edward Diggens, who fought in the Battle of Somme, was auctioned off in early 2020. ("Soldier's World War One diary discovered in Leicestershire barn," BBC News, BBC, February 3, 2020, accessed on March 19, 2020, https://www.bbc.com/news/uk-england-leicestershire-51356195.)

away. Like the films by Jackson and Mendes, each director had a personal connection in bringing these stories to light. Peter Jackson dedicated his film, *They Shall Not Grow Old*, to his grandfather who had served in the Great War. Sam Mendes dedicated and based some of the scenes of the film, *1917*, to his grandfather Lance Corporal Alfred H. Mendes who had "told us the stories." For both directors, the films were more than re-telling a story instead they offered an opportunity for them to have deep personal connections in order to understand their grandfathers' experience in the Great War. The films are a great reminder that history is never unbiased. Great work and scholarship can arise when a person places a deep personal connection within their research to create a thought-provoking piece of work for the public.

Six years ago, I began this journey on my grandparent's couch with a simple question that was asked from my mother. My journey led me to examine my great-grandfather's step by step experiences in the Meuse Argonne Offensive. It also allowed me to examine my grandfather's own experience in the United States Army and how it was different than James. It allowed me to discover how to transcribe and preserve one-hundred-year-old documents. In my journey, I was also able to discover new pieces of evidence like the letters and photographs from James' time in the United States Army. In my oral interviews, I was able to connect with my own grandfather and ask him about valuable moments in his life. My journey allowed me to open my own past and see the connections with my great-grandfather, a man that I had never met.

I was also fortunate to learn more about my great-grandparents and their relationship together. It was a rewarding experience to learn how well they treated each other and had a deep love that no words can ever describe. The oral interviews with my grandfather allowed me to learn about the later parts of their lives and how they stood steadfast in taking care of each other. One of the deepest parts of this thesis was my great-grandfather's mission to take care of my great-grandmother, even in his old age. He would not let anything tear them apart, even if it meant sacrificing his own long-term health in the process. It was like he had to repay Evelyn for all the time they missed while he was overseas. They were deeply devoted to each other. James wrote in the diary that he would often picture himself as an old veteran "relating my war stories over and over again adding some to it every time to make it all the more exciting"[146] and Evelyn sitting by old and gray, knitting away. I would like to think of my great-grandfather sitting in heaven adding to his war stories, while Evelyn sits right next to him, knitting away.

---

[146] James A. Bowman. *Diary, 1918-1919*. Transcribed by Cheryl Foy and Alexander Foy.

# REFERENCES

Allen, Hervey. *Toward the Flame.* New York: George H. Doran Co.43, 1926.

Ambda, Saladin. "Woodrow Wilson: Campaigns and Elections," Miller Center, University of Virginia, September 12, 2019, https://millercenter.org/president/wilson/campaigns-and-elections.

American Battle Monuments Commission, *1st division, summary of operations in the World War.* Washington, D.C.: U.S. Government Printing Office, 1944.

Ancestry.com. *U.S., Department of Veterans Affairs BIRLS Death File, 1850-2010* [database on-line]. Provo, UT, USA: Ancestry.com Operations, Inc., 2011.

Ancestry.com. *U.S., World War I Draft Registration Cards, 1917-1918* [database on-line]. Provo, UT, USA: Ancestry.com Operations Inc, 2005.

Ayres, Leonard P. *The War With Germany: A Statistical Summary.* Washington, D.C.: Government Printing Office, 1919.

Bowman, Evelyn, "Letter to James Bowman (1918)", transcribed by Cheryl Foy. (Private collection of Alexander Foy, 2020).

Bowman, James A. Diary, *1918-1919.* Transcribed by Cheryl Foy and Alexander Foy.

Bowman, James A. "Letters to Evelyn Bowman." Transcribed by Cheryl Foy. (Private collection of Alexander Foy, 2020).

Bowman, Robert. interview by Alexander Foy, February 27, 2017.

Bowman, Robert. interview by Alexander Foy, November 14, 2017.

Bowman, Robert, interview by Alexander Foy, March 8, 2020.

Browder, Dewey. "Schlieffen Plan." *World War I: The Definitive Encyclopedia and Document Collection*, 2014, 1430-432.

Buchbinder, R. 2004. *Plantar Fasciitis. The New England Journal of Medicine*. Vol. 350.

Buffum, Douglas "Origin of the Word 'Boche,'" *Current History: A Monthly Magazine of the New York Times*, Vol. 4 (1916).

Citation from 91st Division. United States Army. (Private collection of Alexander Foy, 2020).

Collins, Ross F. 2008. *World War I: Primary Documents on Events from 1914 to 1919*. Westport, Conn.: Greenwood Press, 2008.

Connelly, Katie. "Frustration for the US soldiers who never went to war," BBC News, BBC, July 10, 2010, accessed on March 8, 2020, https://www.bbc.com/news/world-us-canada-10547610.

Cram, George F. to his Mother, January 1, 1863, *Soldiering with Sherman: Civil War Letters of George F. Cram*, ed. Jennifer Cain Bohrnstedt. DeKalb, IL: 2000.

Davies, Edward A. 79th Division, 315 Regiment, WWIS, MHI.

Faulkner, Richard Shawn. *Meuse-Argonne 26 September-11 November 1918*. U.S. Army Campaigns of World War I, 2018.

Ferrell, Robert H. *America's Deadliest Battle: Meuse-Argonne, 1918*. Lawrence, Kansas: University Press of Kansas, 2007.

Fussell, Paul. *The Great War and Modern Memory*. Oxford Univ. Press Pbk. ed. Galaxy Book; GB483. London; New York: Oxford University Press, 1977.

Hickey, Alice. "The Need for War Letters?" (2008). *Undergraduate Humanities Forum 2007-2008*: Origins. 6. http://repository.upenn.edu/uhf_2008/6.

"Hindenburg Line." *The Oxford Essential Dictionary of the U.S. Military*, 2001, The Oxford Essential Dictionary of the U.S. Military.

Hunt, Nigel C., *Memory, War and Trauma*. Leiden: Cambridge University Press, 2010.

Keene, Jennifer. *American Soldiers' Lives: World War I*. Westport, CT: Greenwood Press, 2006.

Lovegren, Sylvia. "Bully Beef." *The Oxford Encyclopedia of Food and Drink in America*, 2004, The Oxford Encyclopedia of Food and Drink in America.

Lurati, Ann. 2015. "Flat Feet and a Diagnosis of Plantar Fasciitis in a Marine Corps Recruit." *Workplace Health & Safety* 63 (4): 136–38. https://doi.org/10.1177/2165079915576923.

Manufacture de Caoutchouc Michelin. *Battle of the Marne*. Michelin & Co.: 1917, http://hdl.handle.net/2027/coo.31924005794411.

Mastriano, Douglas. *Thunder in the Argonne: A New History of America's Greatest Battle*. Kentucky: University Press of Kentucky, 2018.

Meriam-Webster Dictionaries, s.v. "grit" accessed September 12, 2019, https://www.merriam-webster.com/dictionary/grit.

Meuse-Argonne Offensive, September 26 to November 11, 1918, Scenes of Traffic Conditions, 1936; Record Group 111: Records of the Office of the Chief Signal Officer, 1860 – 1985; Historical Films, ca. 1914 - ca. 1936; National Archives at College Park - Motion Pictures (RDSM).

Meyer, Jessica. *Men of War: Masculinity and the First World War in Britain*. Genders and Sexualities in History. Basingstoke [England]; New York: Palgrave Macmillan, 2009.

Nichols, Vernon. “Our Battle of the Argonne.” Infantry Journal no. 16 (September 1919).

“Nottingham soldier's war diary goes under the hammer,” BBC News, BBC, December 12, 2019, accessed on March 19, 2020, https://www.bbc.com/news/uk-england-nottinghamshire-50758400.

Patrick, Neil. “The connection between Ace of spades and war- it was used for good luck but also as a psychological weapon,” The Vintage News. Timera Media, July 24, 2016, Accessed December 14, 2019, https://www.thevintagenews.com/2016/07/24/ace-spades-connection-war-used-good-luck-also-psychological-weapon-2/.

Pendergast, Tom, Sara Slovey, Sara Pendergast, and Christine Slovey. *World War I*. Detroit, Mich.: U.X.L., 2002.

Photograph No. 20805710. “American Red Cross - Miscellaneous - American Red Cross furnishes chocolate. Close up of hand grasping chocolate showing label “Compliments of the American Red Cross” A.R.C. Field Hospital No. 328, 82nd Div., Varenne-en-Argonne, Meuse, France.” March 1919; Records of the War Department General and Special Staffs, Record Group 165. National Archives at College Park, College Park, MD.

Richman, Joe and Samara Freemark, "The Bonus Army: How a Protest Led To The GI Bill," National Public Radion (NPR), National Public Radio (NPR), September 11, 2011, https://www.npr.org/2011/11/11/142224795/the-bonus-army-how-a-protest-led-to-the-gi-bill.

Rosenthal, Elisabeth. 1990. "The Maligned Flat Foot: Some See an Advantage." *New York Times (1923-Current File)*, 1990. http://search.proquest.com/docview/108456559/.

"Soldier's World War One diary discovered in Leicestershire barn," BBC News, BBC, February 3, 2020, accessed on March 19, 2020, https://www.bbc.com/news/uk-england-leicestershire-51356195.

Spickelmier, Roger K. "Training of the American Soldier During World War I and World War II." PhD. diss., U.S. Army Command and General Staff College, 1987.

Strachan, Hew. *The First World War*. Oxford [England]; New York: Oxford University Press, 2001.

Stone, Norman. *World War One*. New York: Basic Books, a Member of the Perseus Books Group, 2009.

Travers, Tim. *World War I: A History*, ed. Hew Strachan. Oxford: Oxford University Press, 1998.

Trickey, Erick. "The Forgotten Story of the American Troops Who Got Caught Up in the Russian Civil War," Smithsonian Magazine, Smithsonian Institute, February 12, 2019, https://www.smithsonianmag.com/history/forgotten-doughboys-who-died-fighting-russian-civil-war-180971470/.

United States Army, "Things they take to war." US Army. Published November 30, 2010. Accessed December 14, 2019, https://www.army.mil/article/48785/things_they_take_to_war.

United States Army. 315th Infantry. *The official history of the 315th Infantry U. S. A.; being a true record of its organization and training, of its operations in the World War, and of its activities following the signing of the armistice. -1919.* [Philadelphia, 1920] Web. https://lccn.loc.gov/20021501.

United States Census Bureau. *Census of Population and Housing, 1880: Statistics of the Population of the United States*. (Washington, D.C: U.S. Government Printing Office, 1880).

United States Census Bureau. *Census of Population and Housing, 1930: Statistics of the Population of the United States*. (Washington, D.C: U.S. Government Printing Office, 1930).

United States, Selective Service System. *World War I Selective Service System Draft Registration Cards, 1917-1918*. (Washington, D.C.: National Archives and Records Administration, 1918). M1509, 4,582 rolls. Imaged from Family History Library microfilm.

Wilson, Bryant and Lamar Tooze. *With the 364th Infantry in America, France and*

*Belgium*. New York: The Knickerbocker Press, 1919.

Wikimedia Commons, "RMS Olympic."

"WW1 pilot's items found in Leicestershire barn 'flabbergasts' expert," BBC News, BBC, February 19, 2020, accessed on March 19, 2020, https://www.bbc.com/news/uk-england-leicestershire-51558511.

91st Division Publication Committee. *The Story of the 91st Division*. San Mateo, CA: H. S. Crocker Co, Inc., 1919.

www.ingramcontent.com/pod-product-compliance
Lightning Source LLC
LaVergne TN
LVHW091310150826
845673LV00006B/1604